Vitality Tattoo
The Tattoo Art of Shannon Schober
Volume I

Vitality Tattoo Volume 1

The Tattoo Art of Shannon Schober

Copyright © 2008

Vitality

1240 Brevard Rd
Suite 1
Asheville NC
28806

ISBN 978-0-9818677-0-0

17 years ago I started my career in tattoo, over this time I have sought to create a body of work that is unique and pleasing to the eye. I offer this collection of photos as representative of my personal approach to this always evolving and vital art form.
Shannon Schober
2008

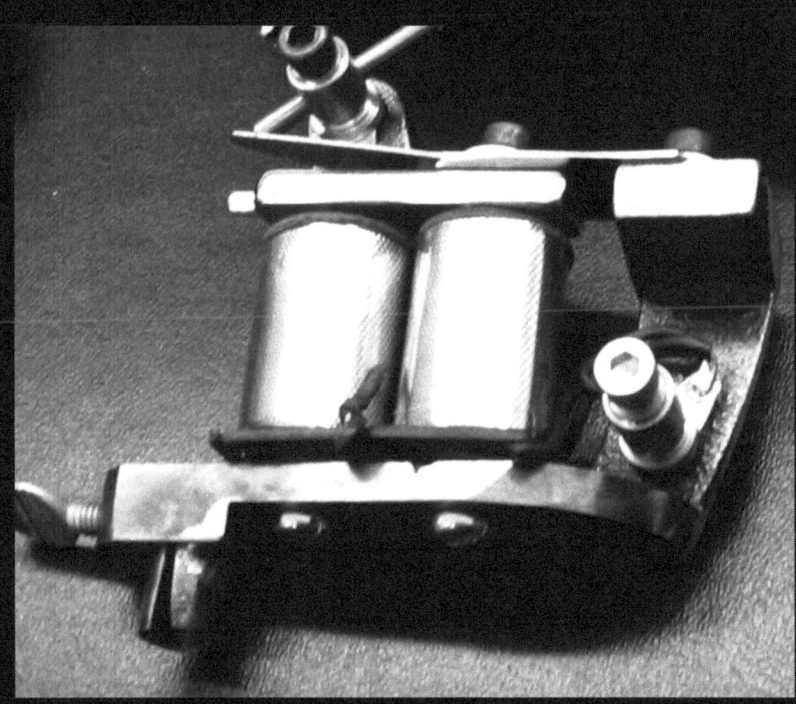

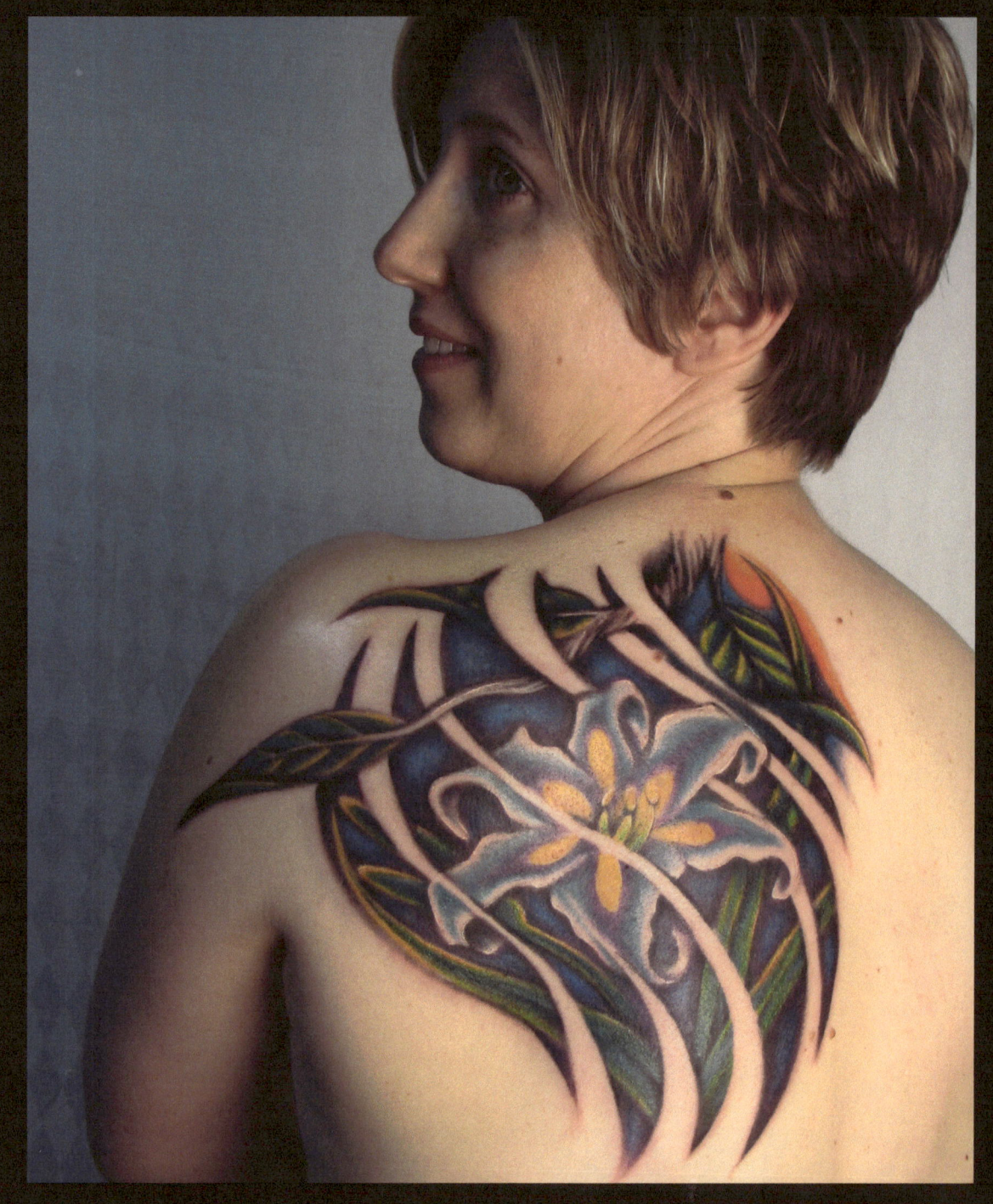

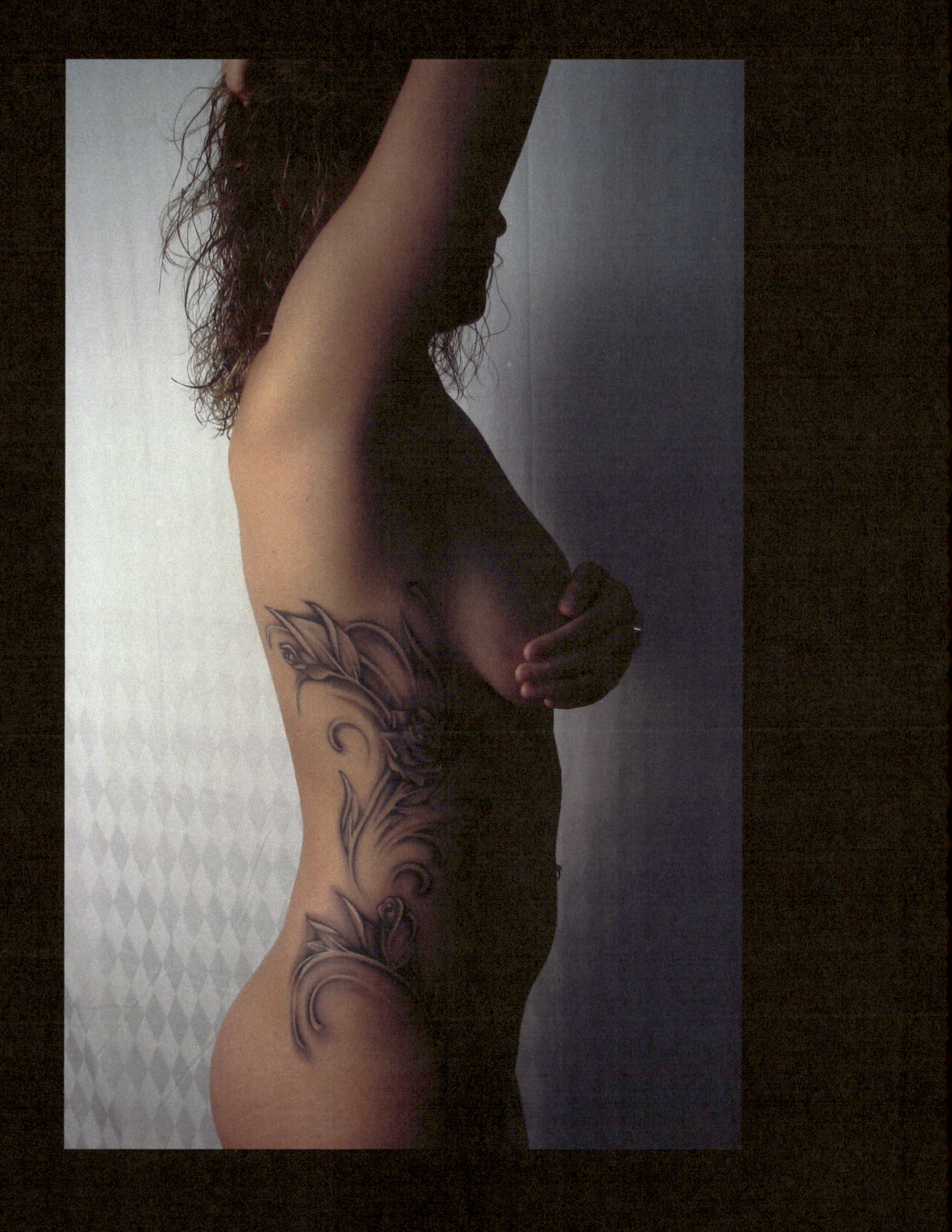

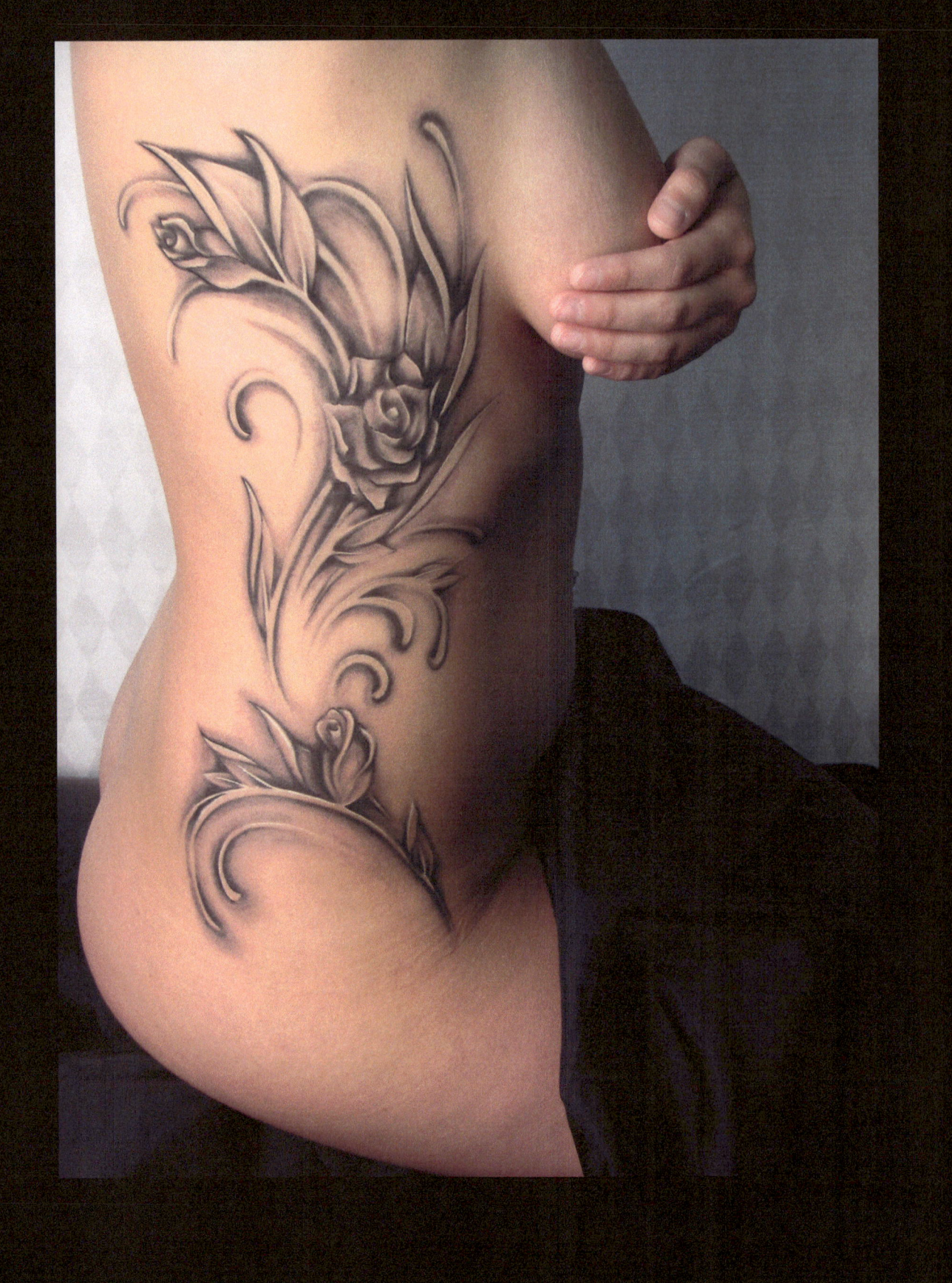

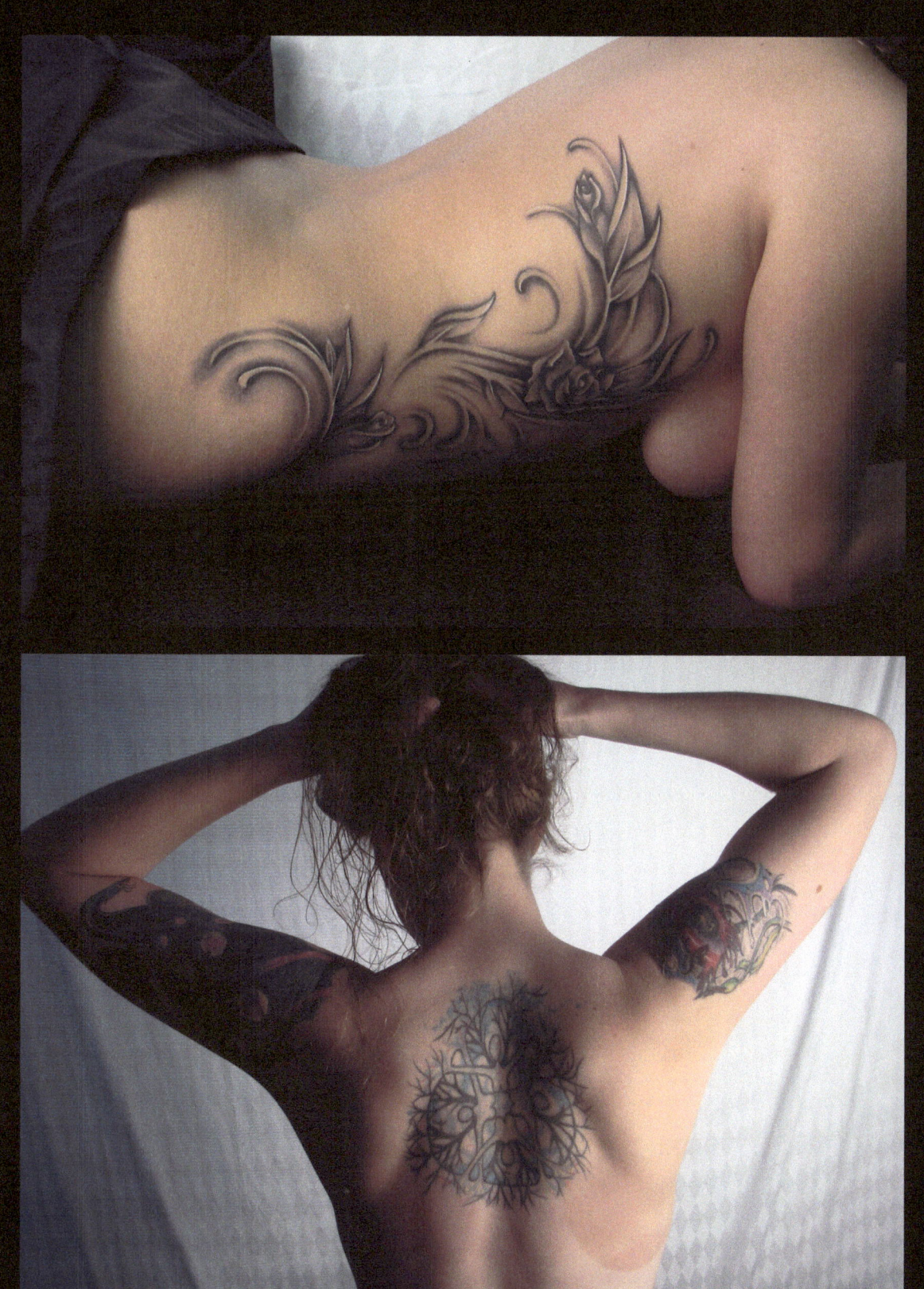

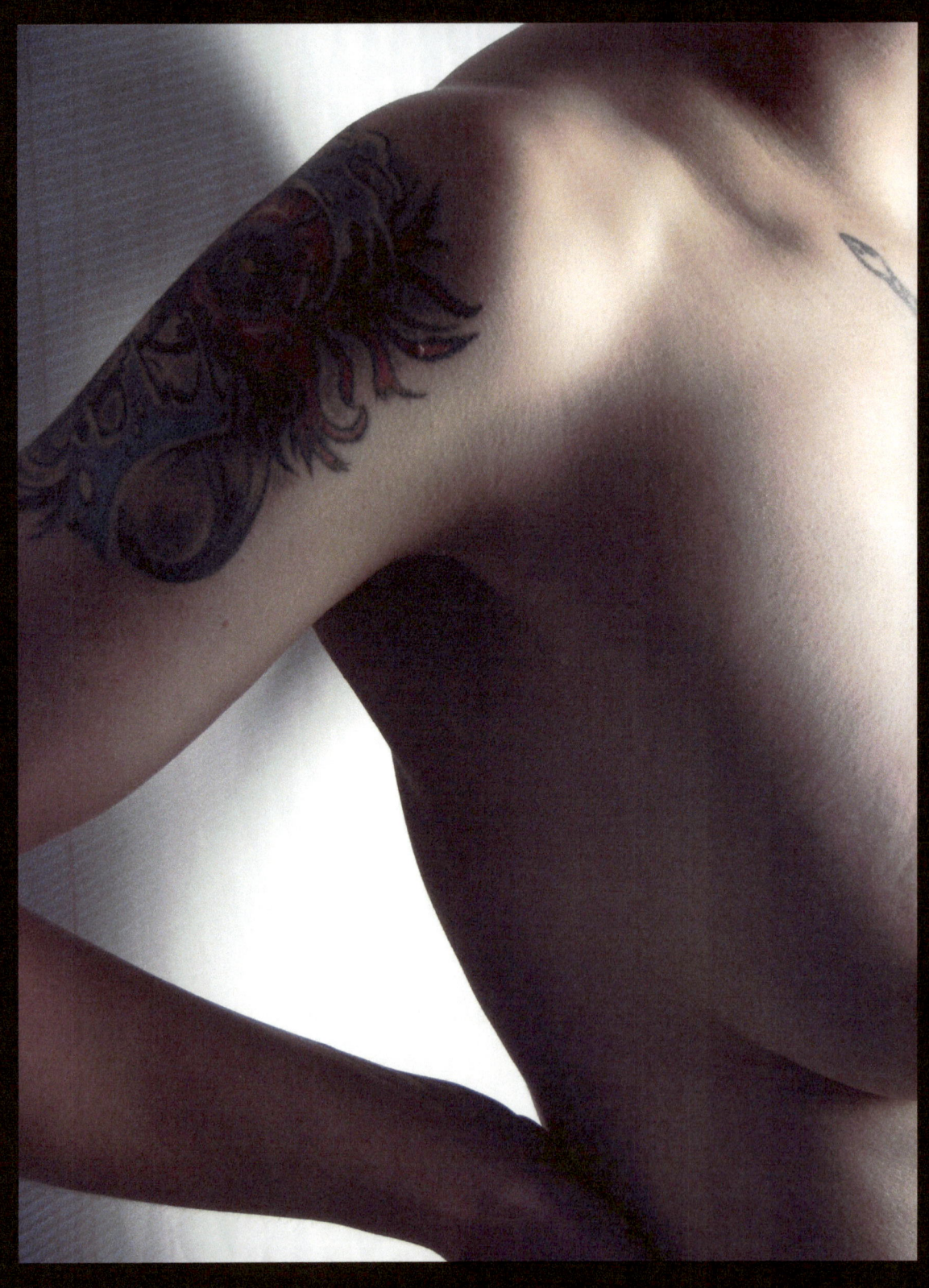

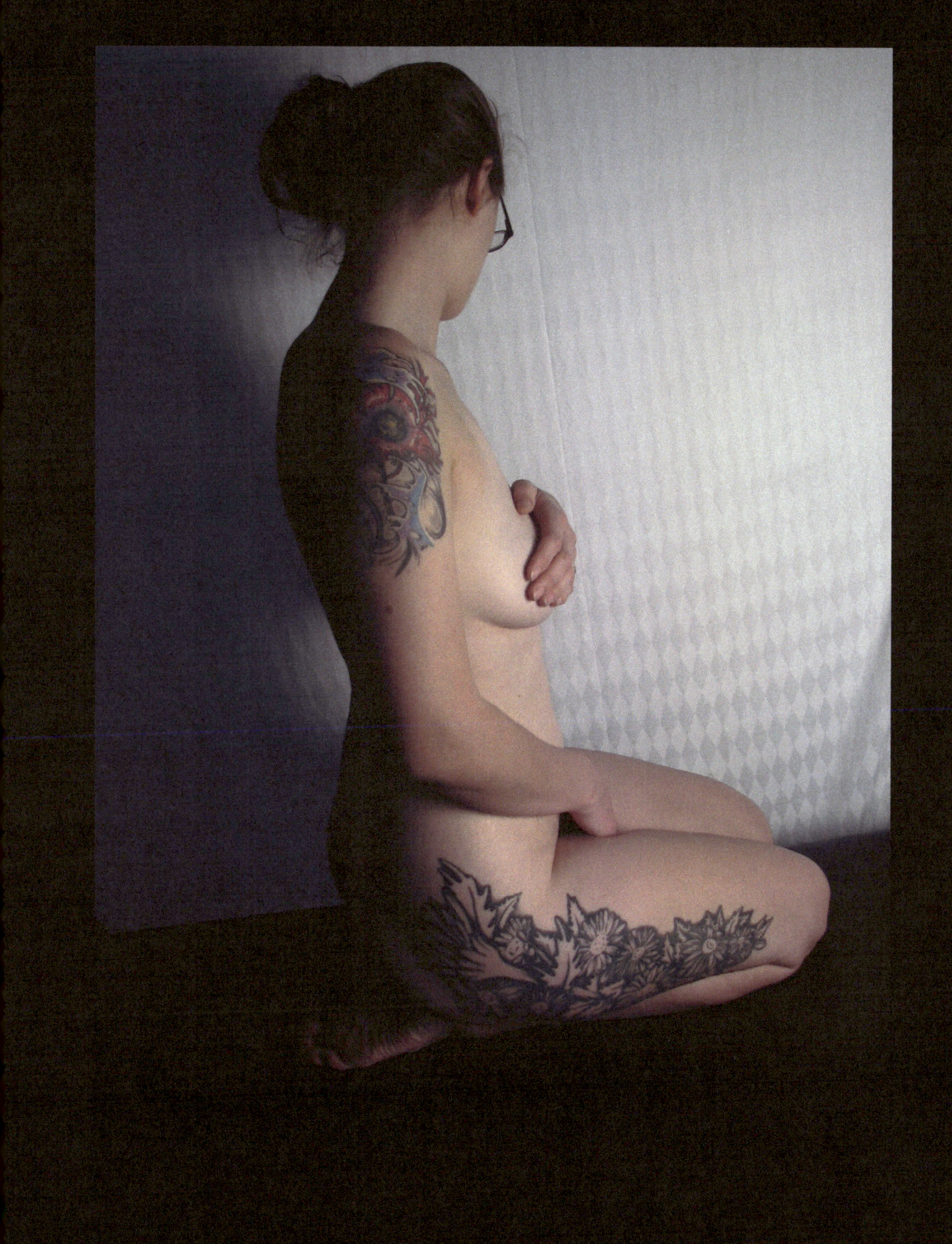

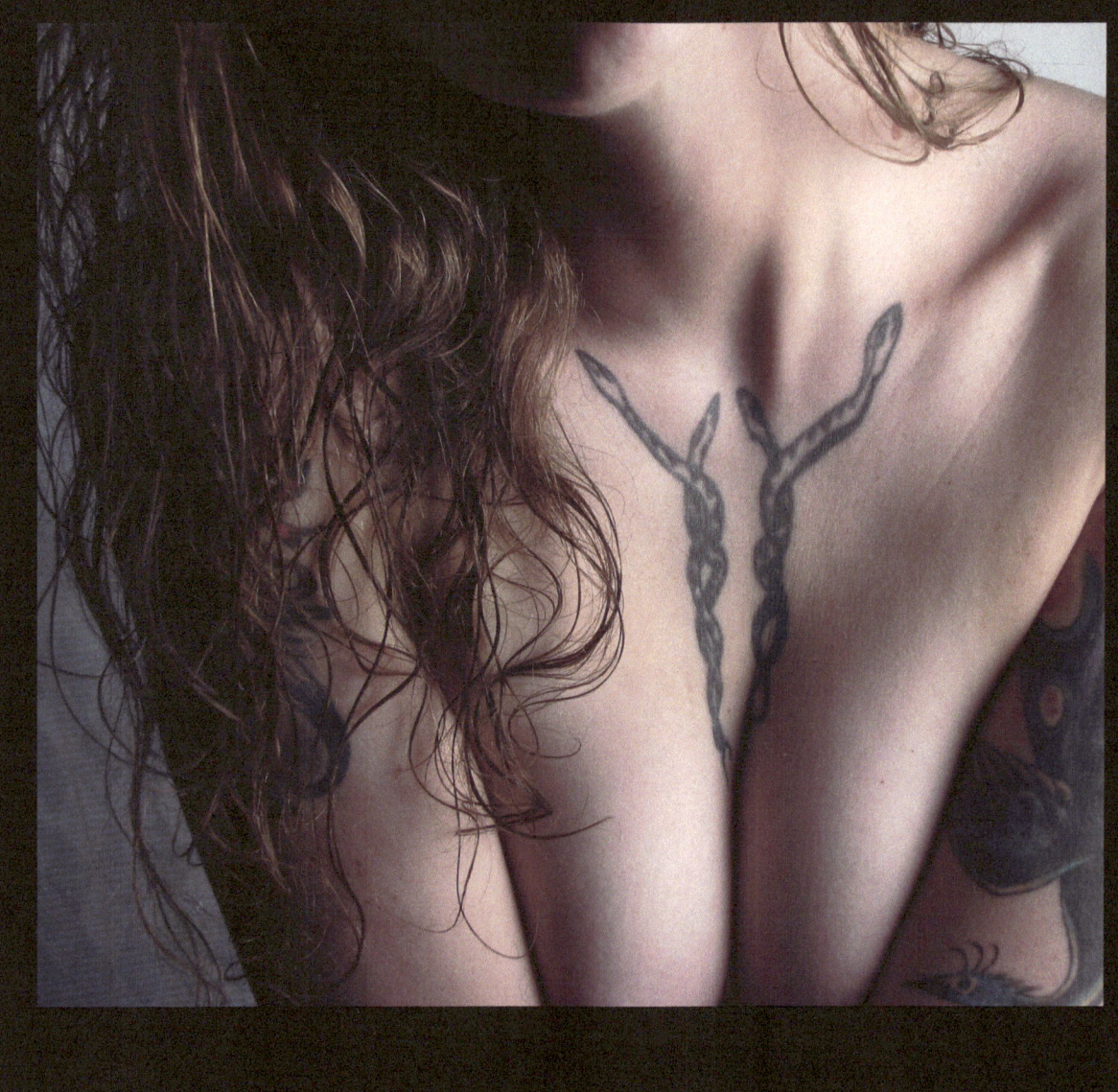

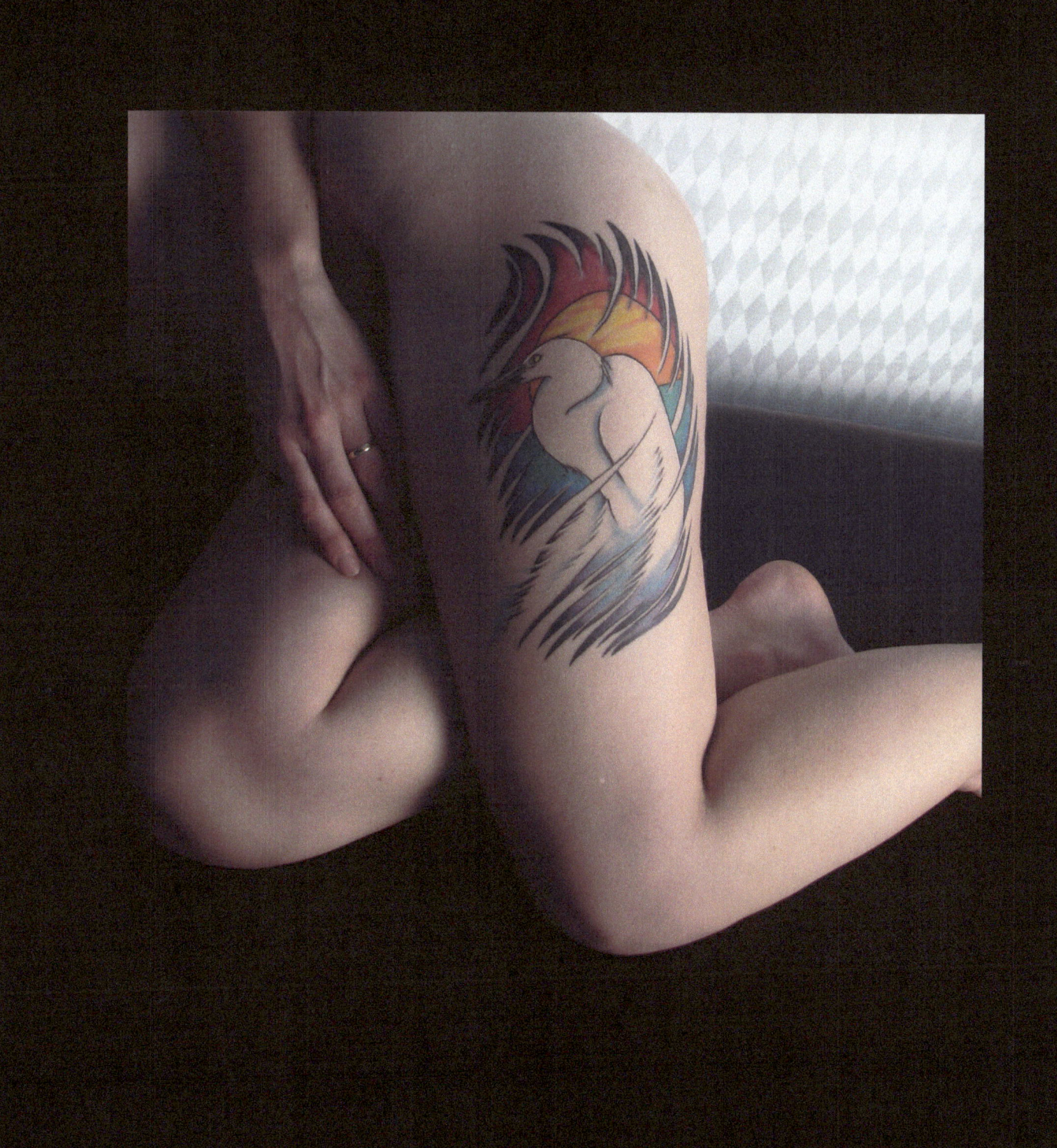

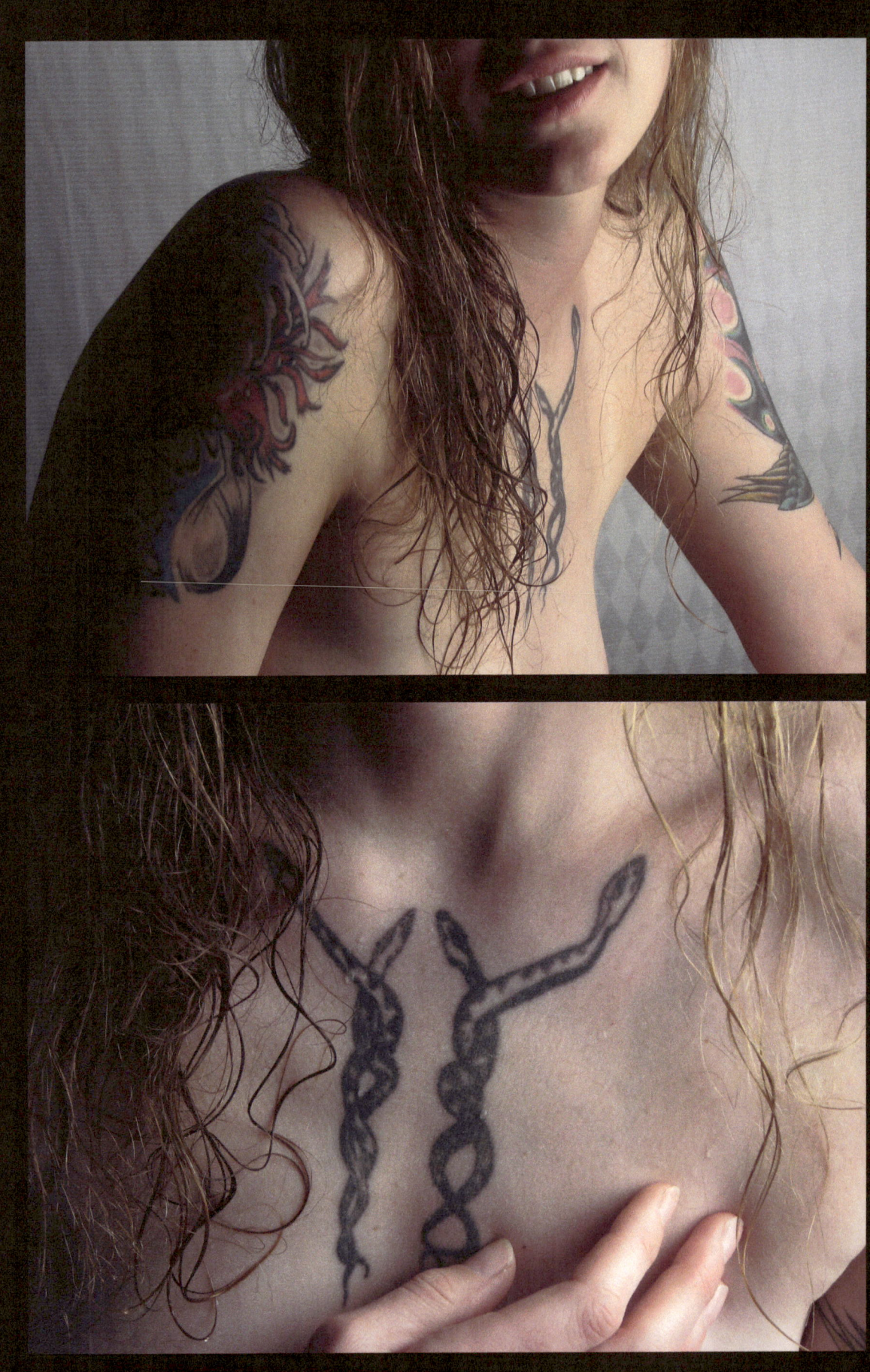

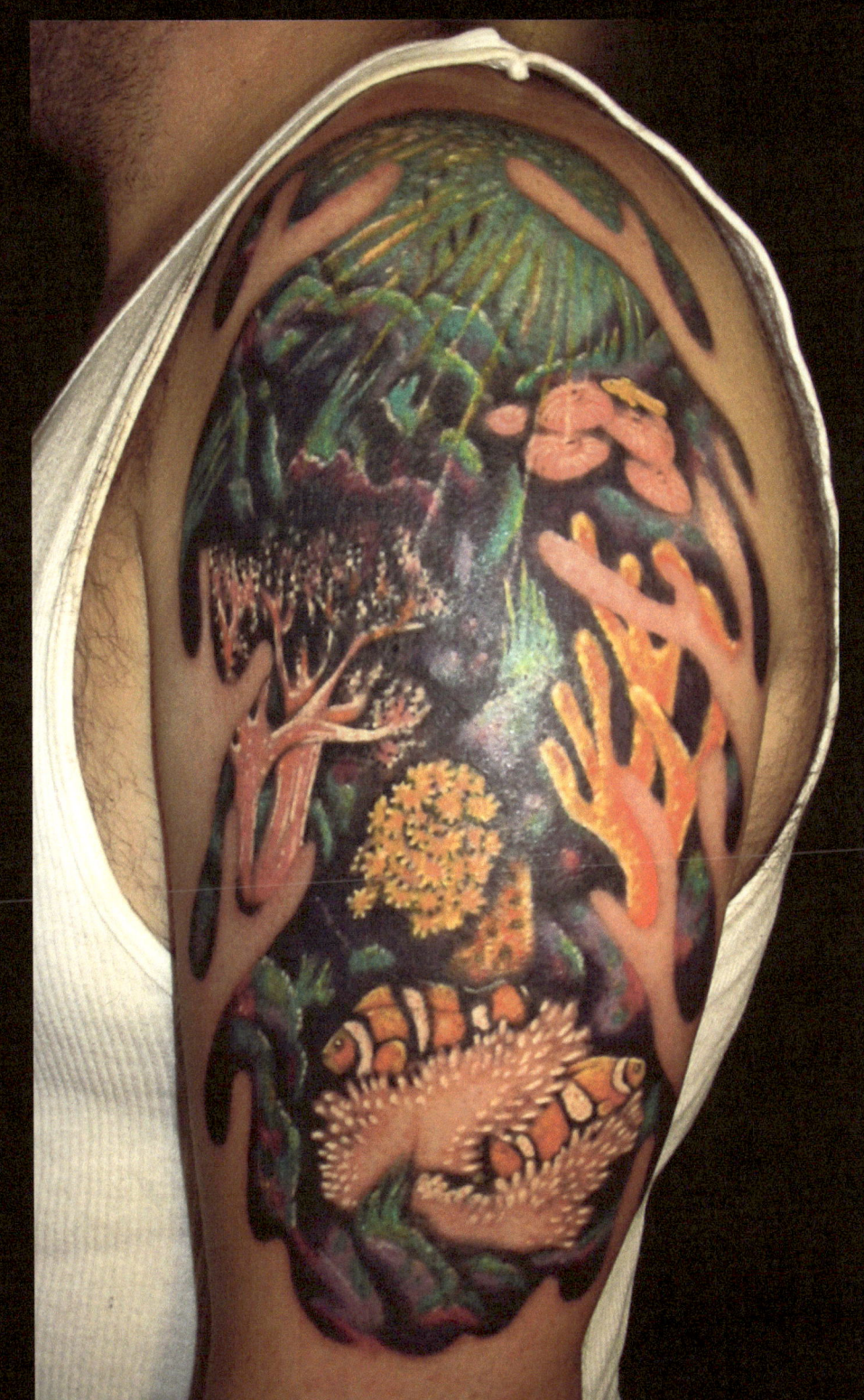

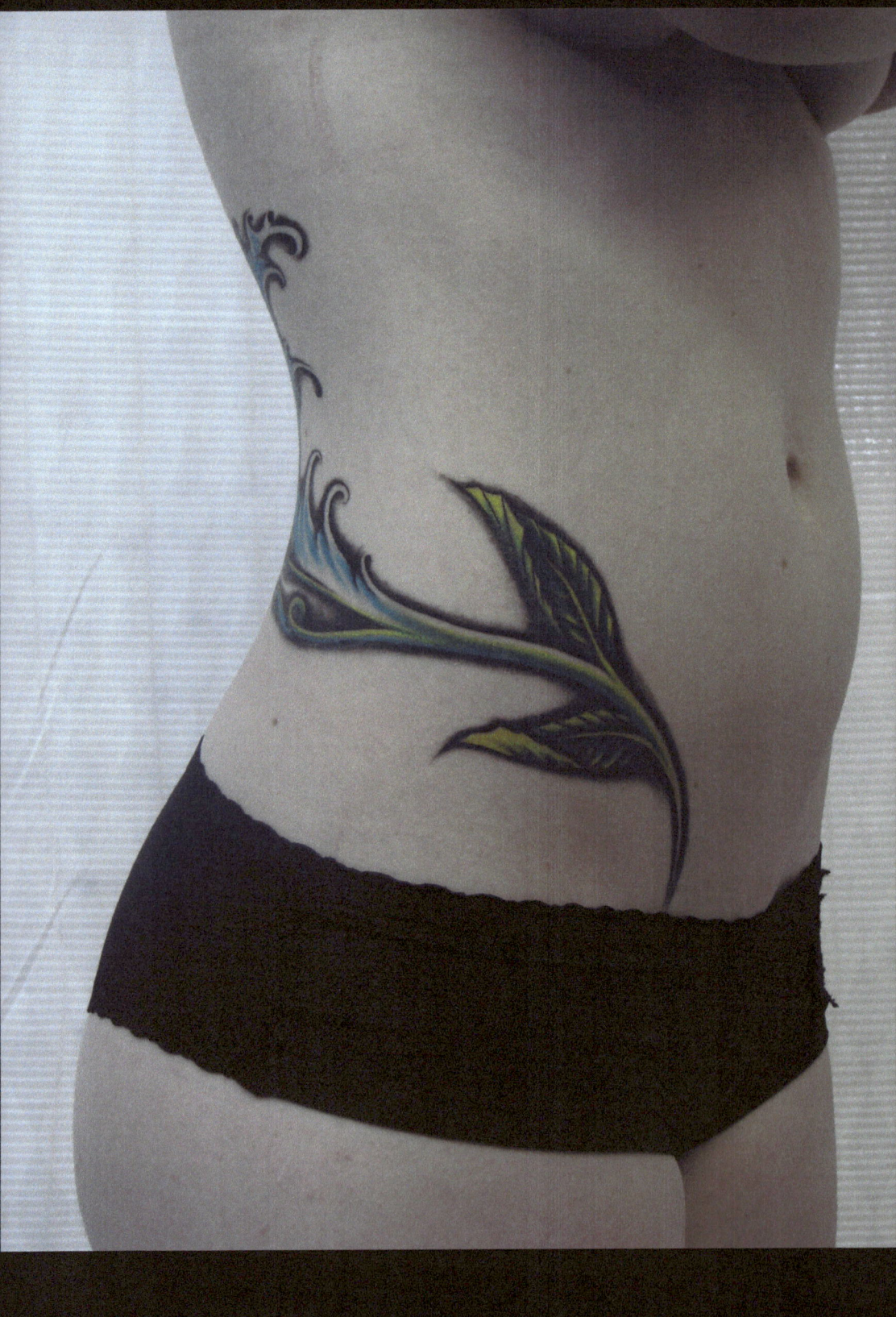

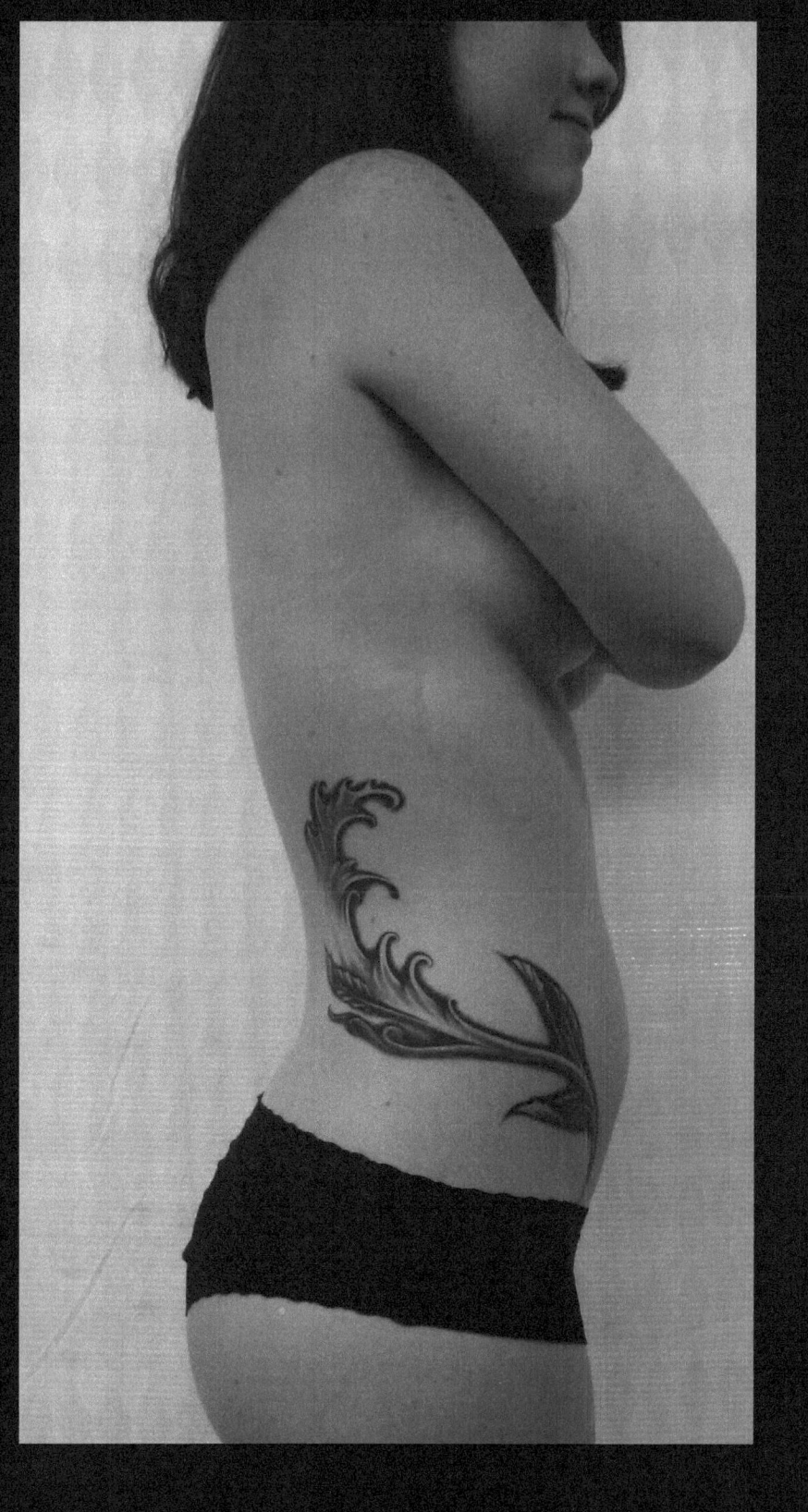

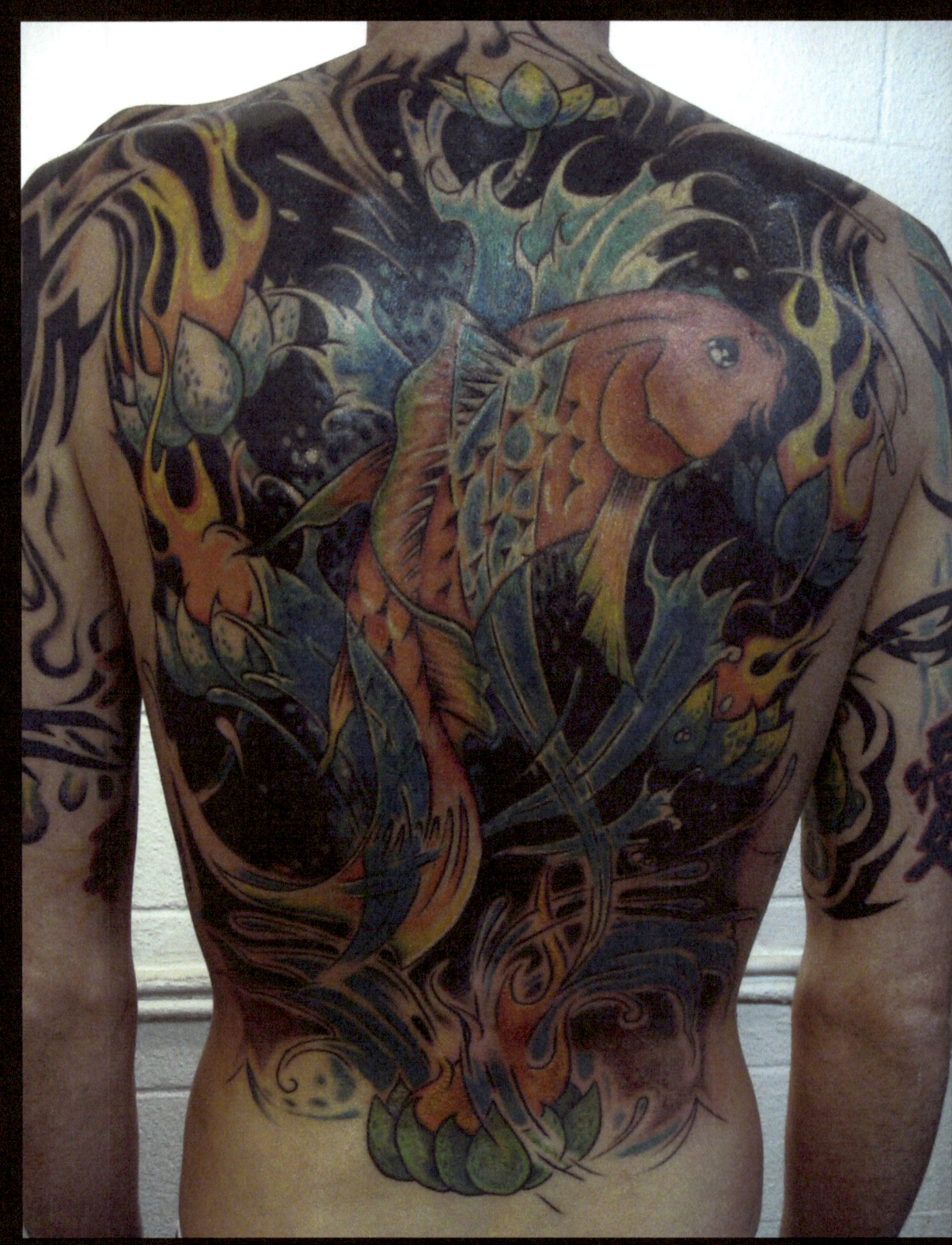

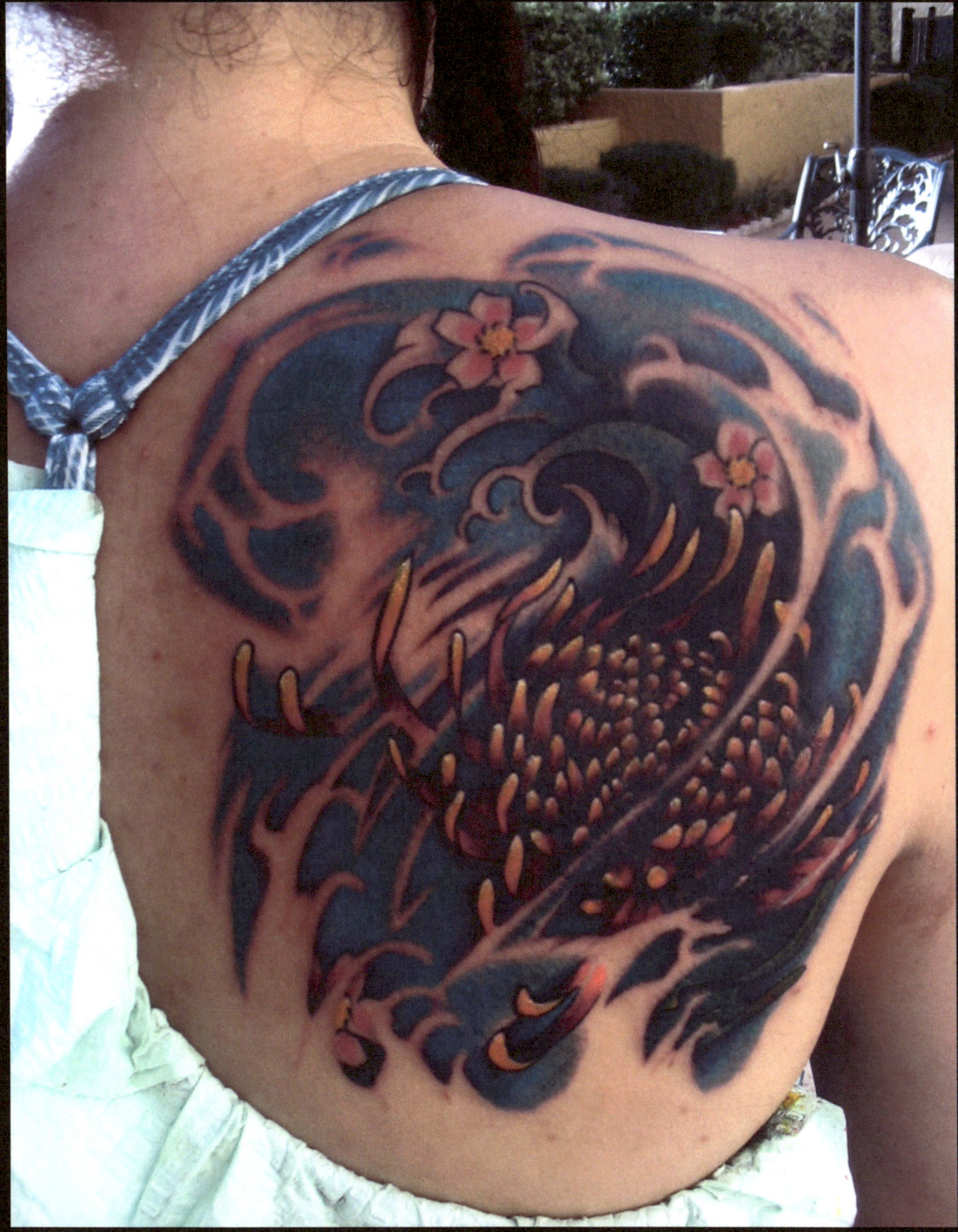

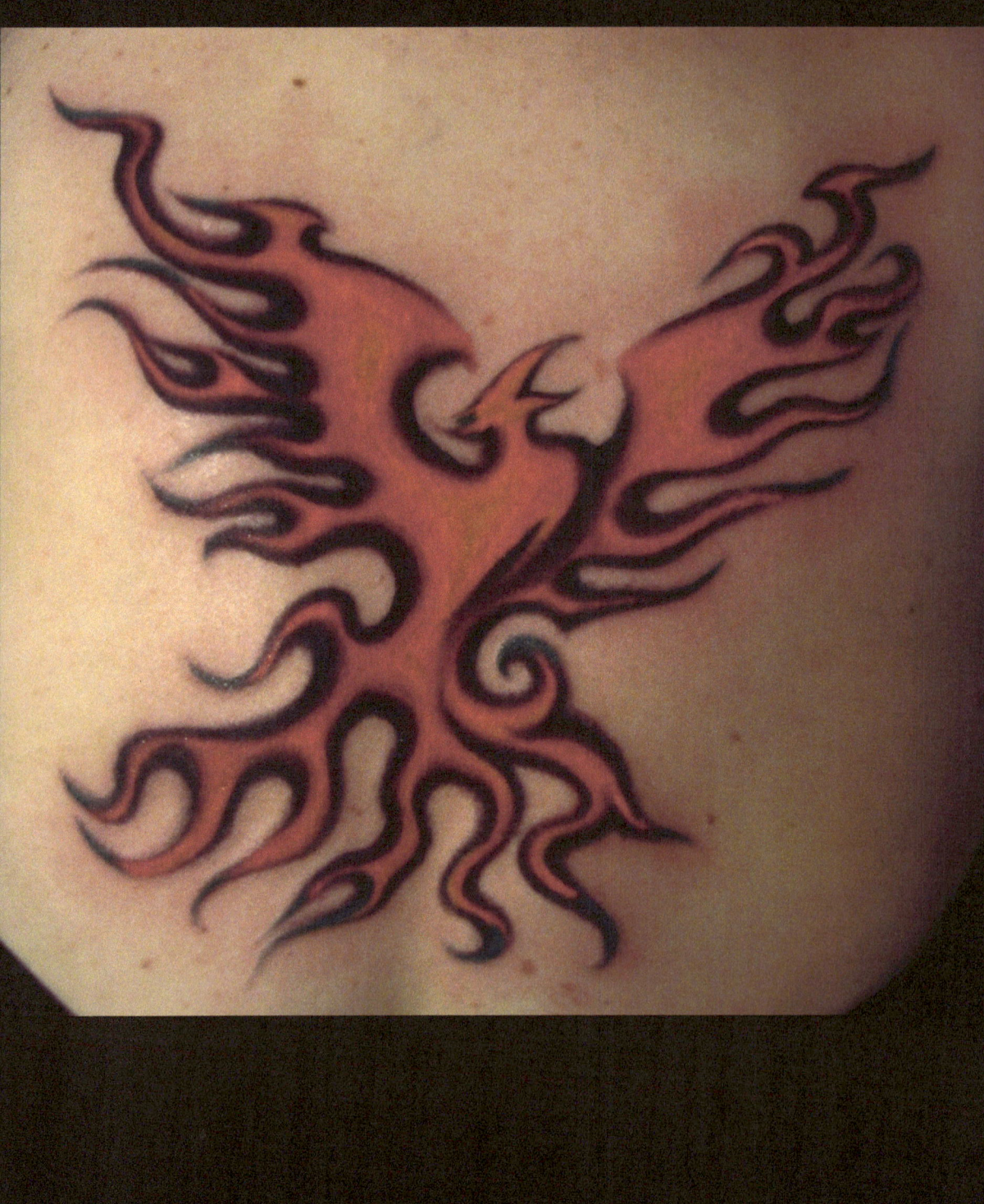

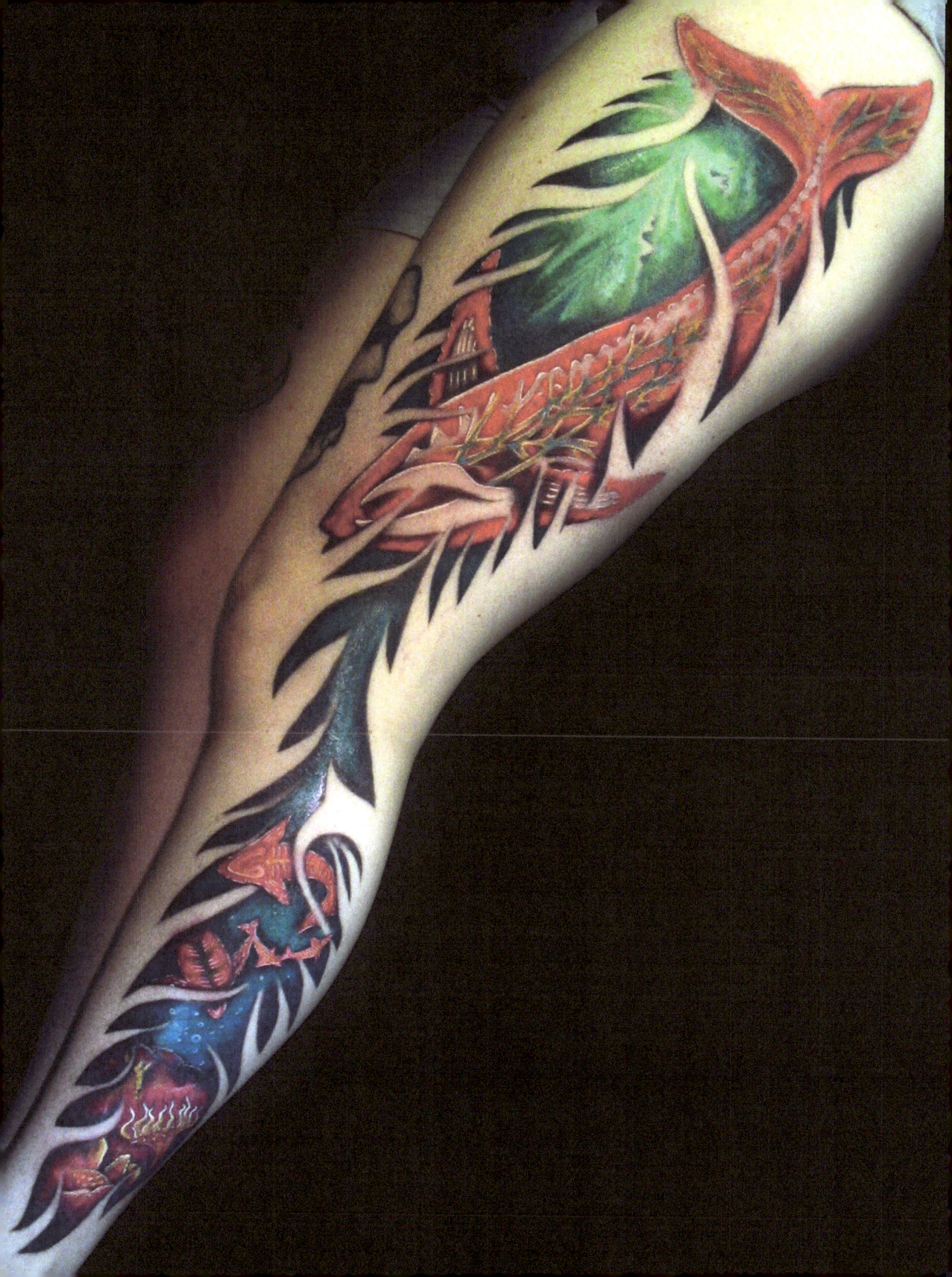

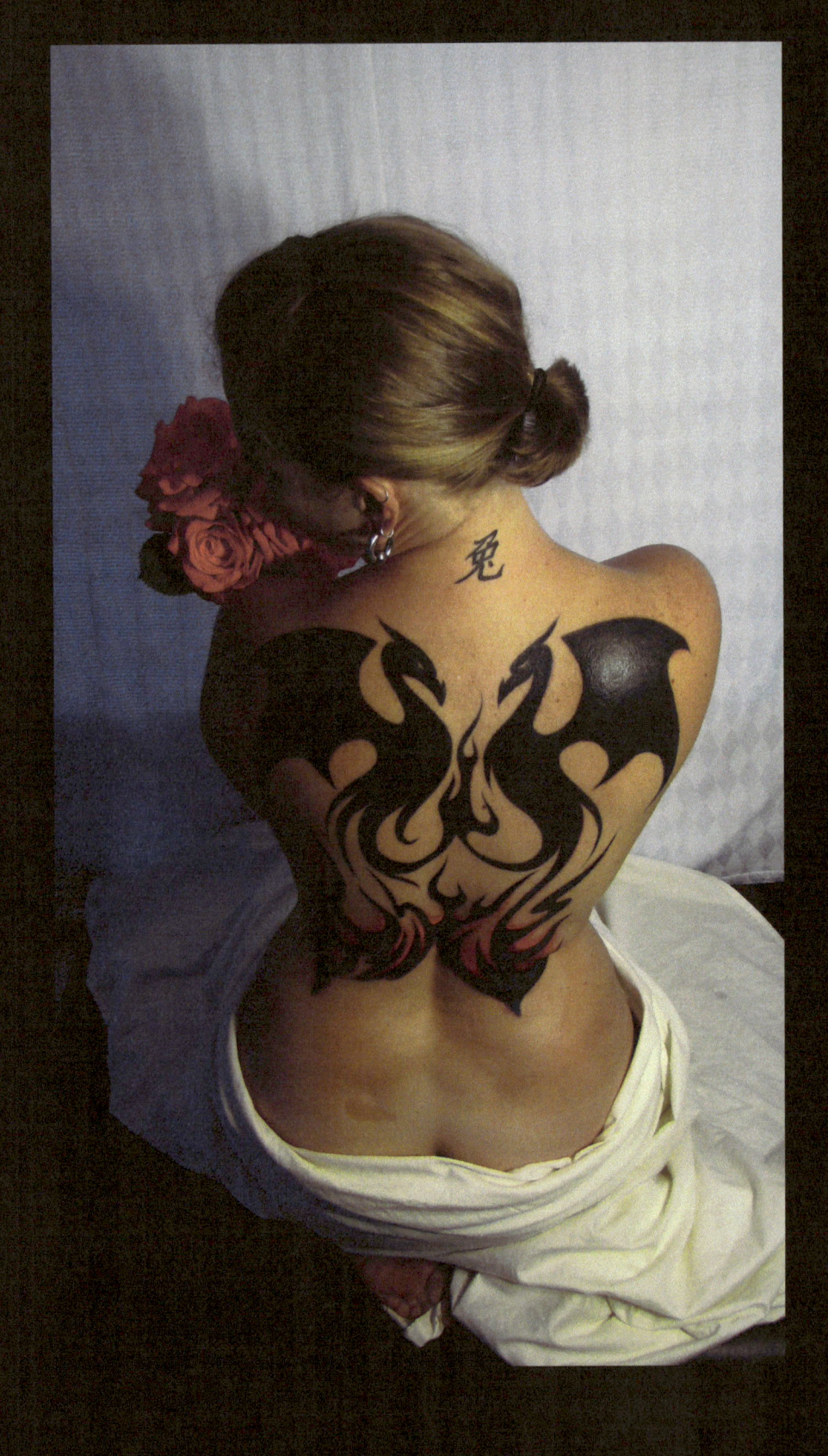

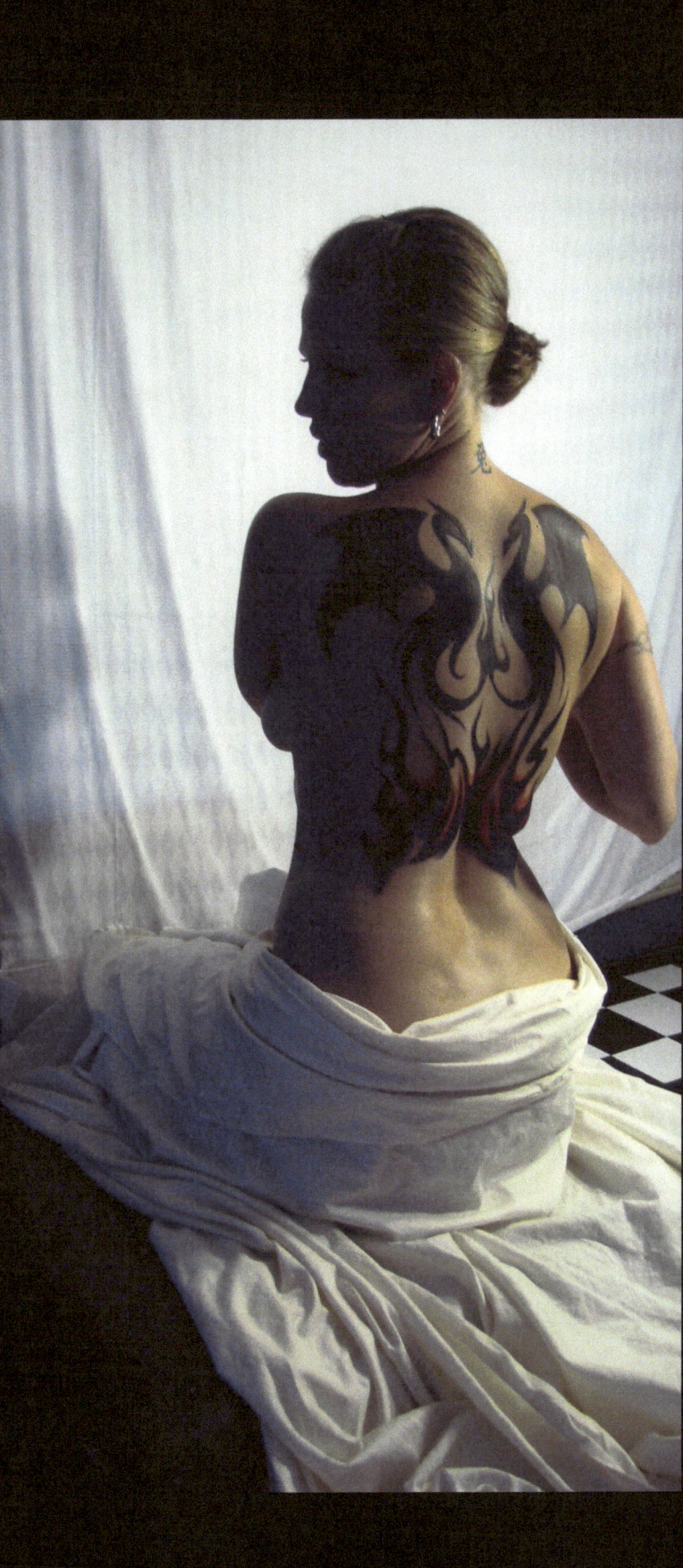

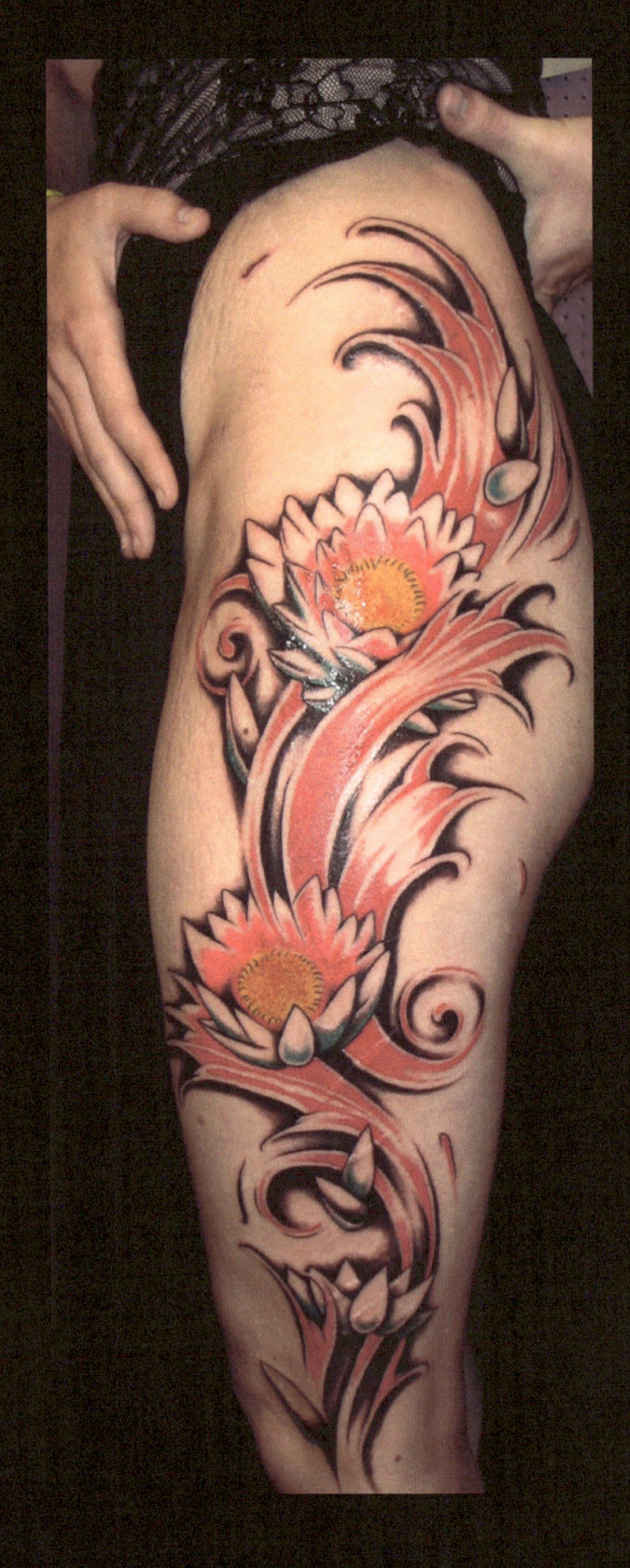

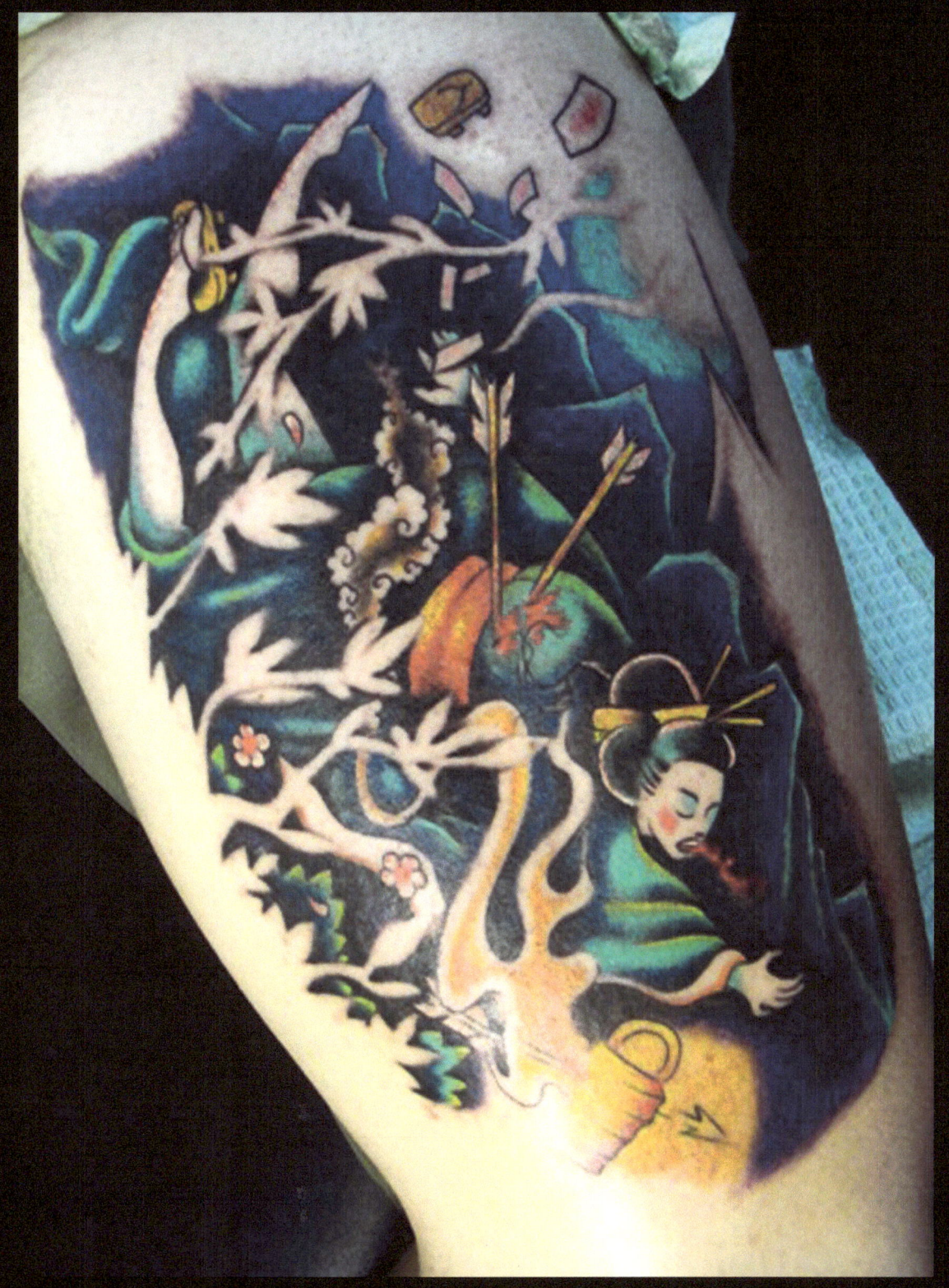

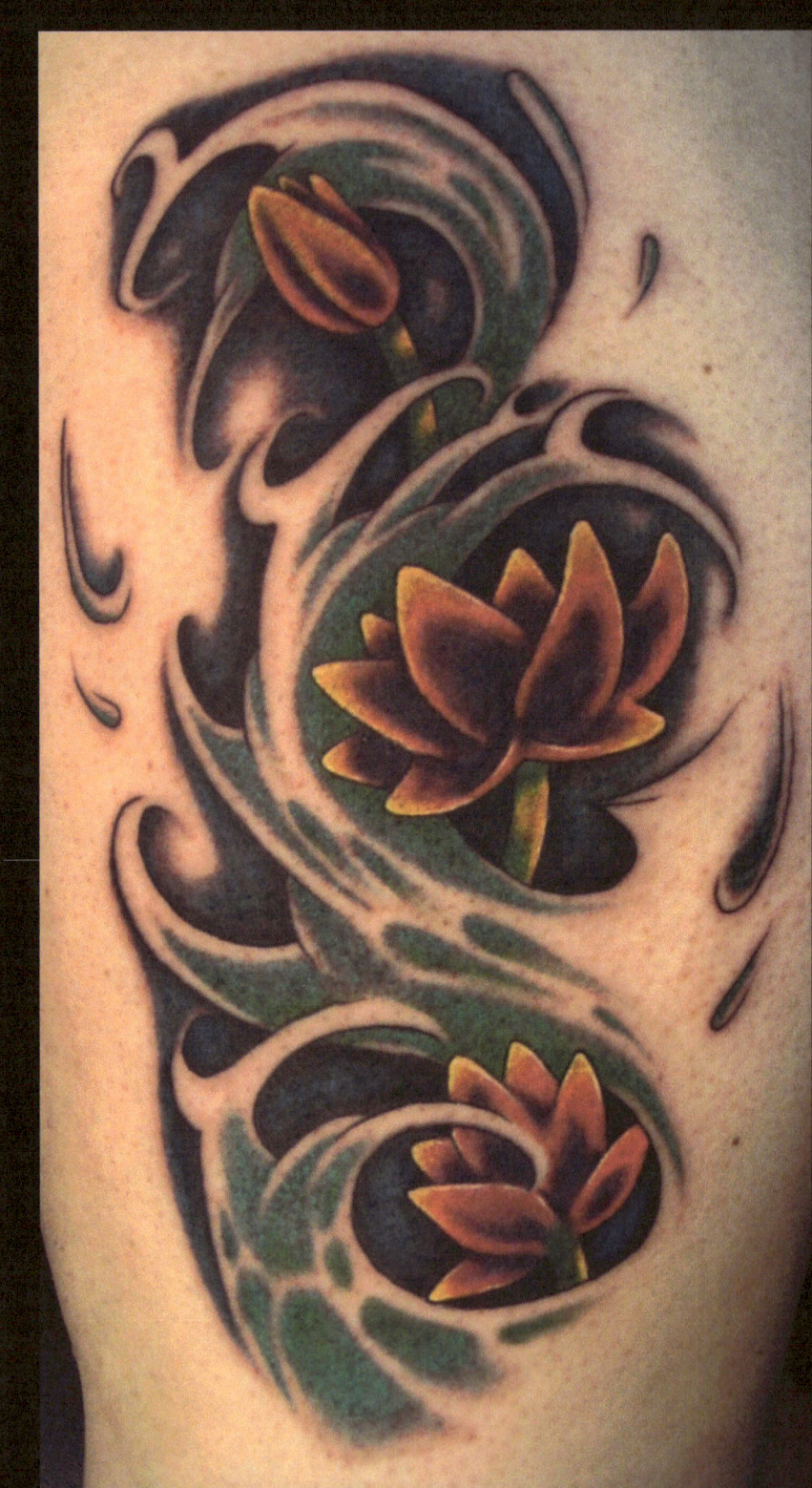

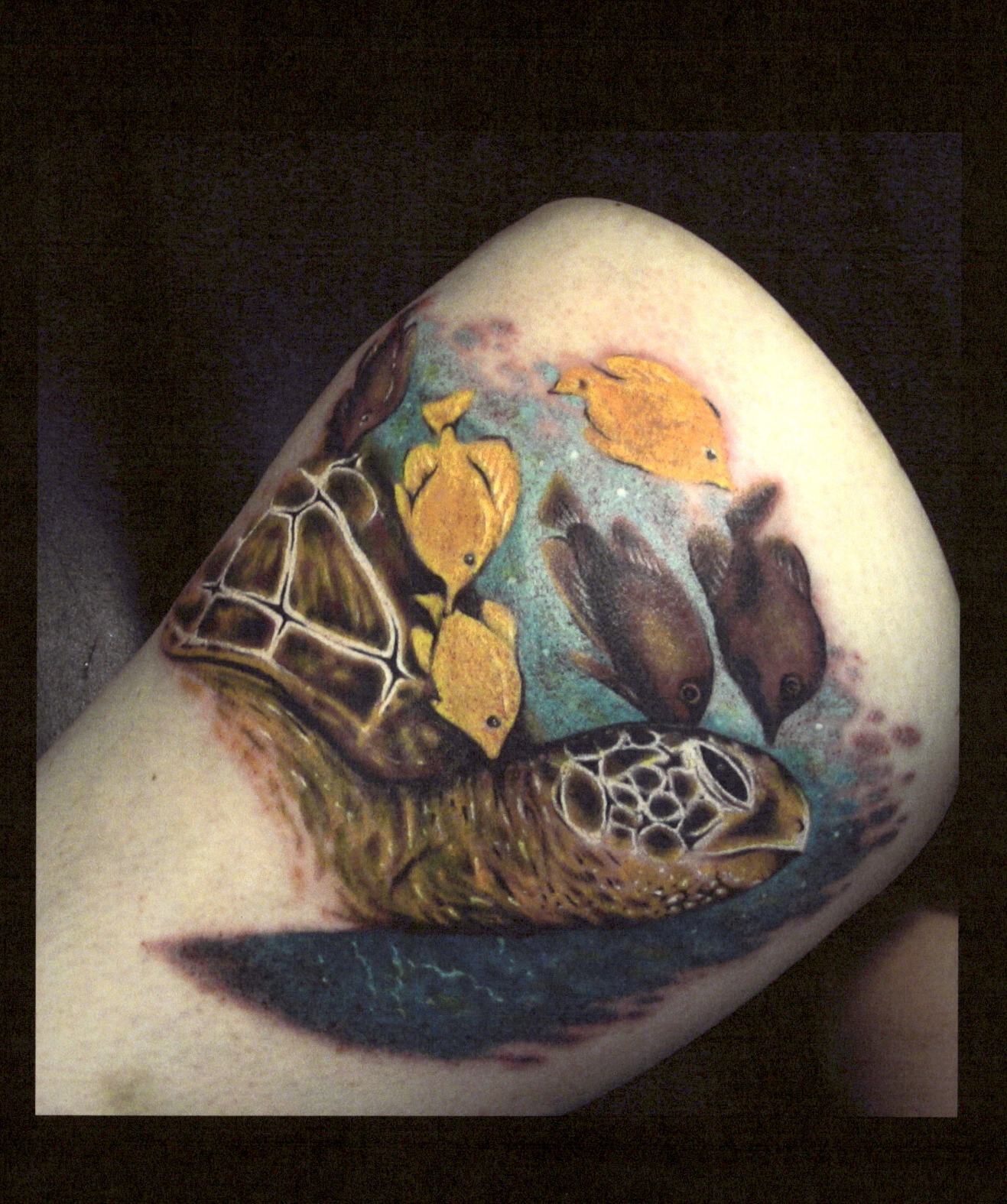

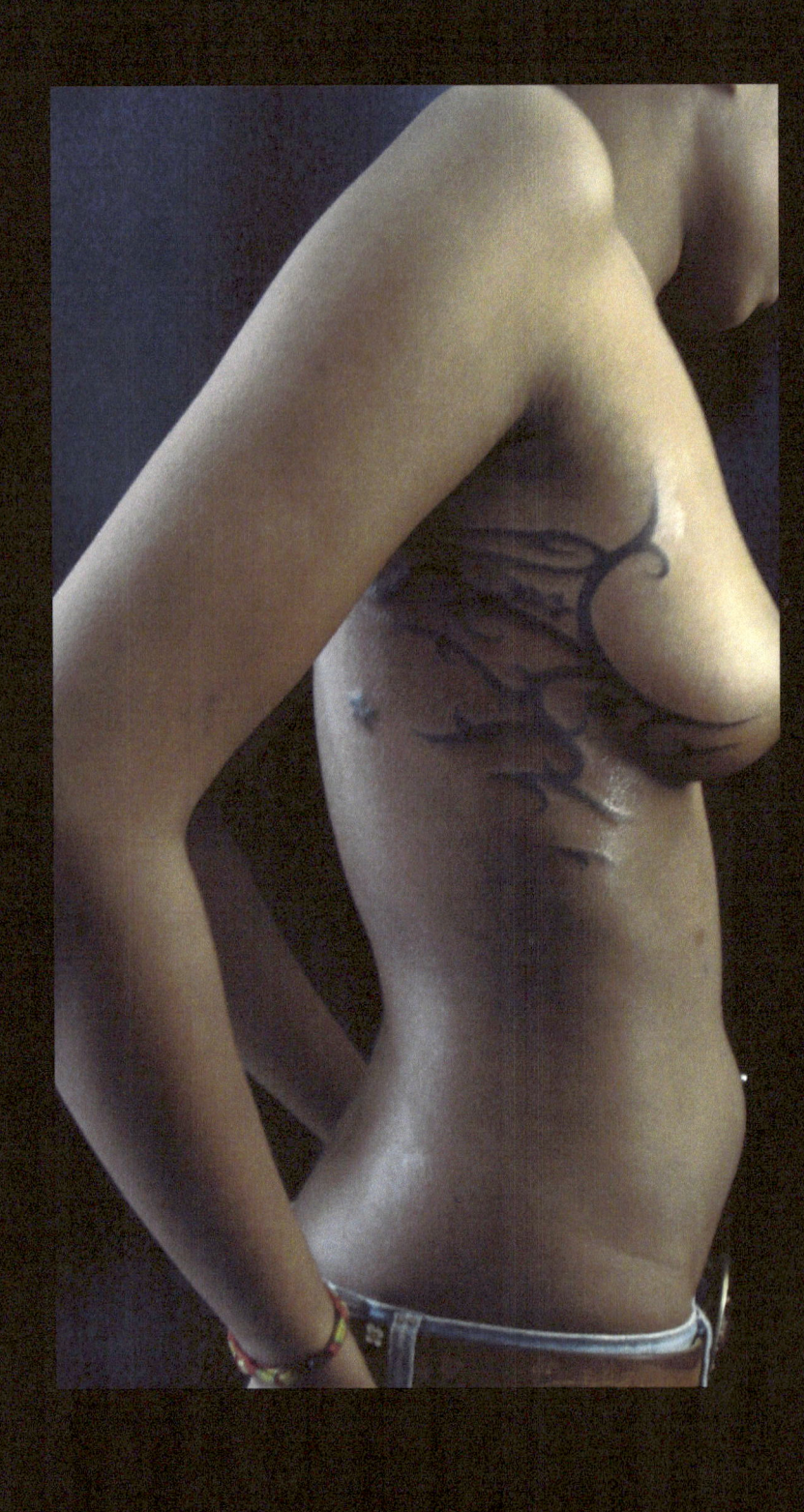

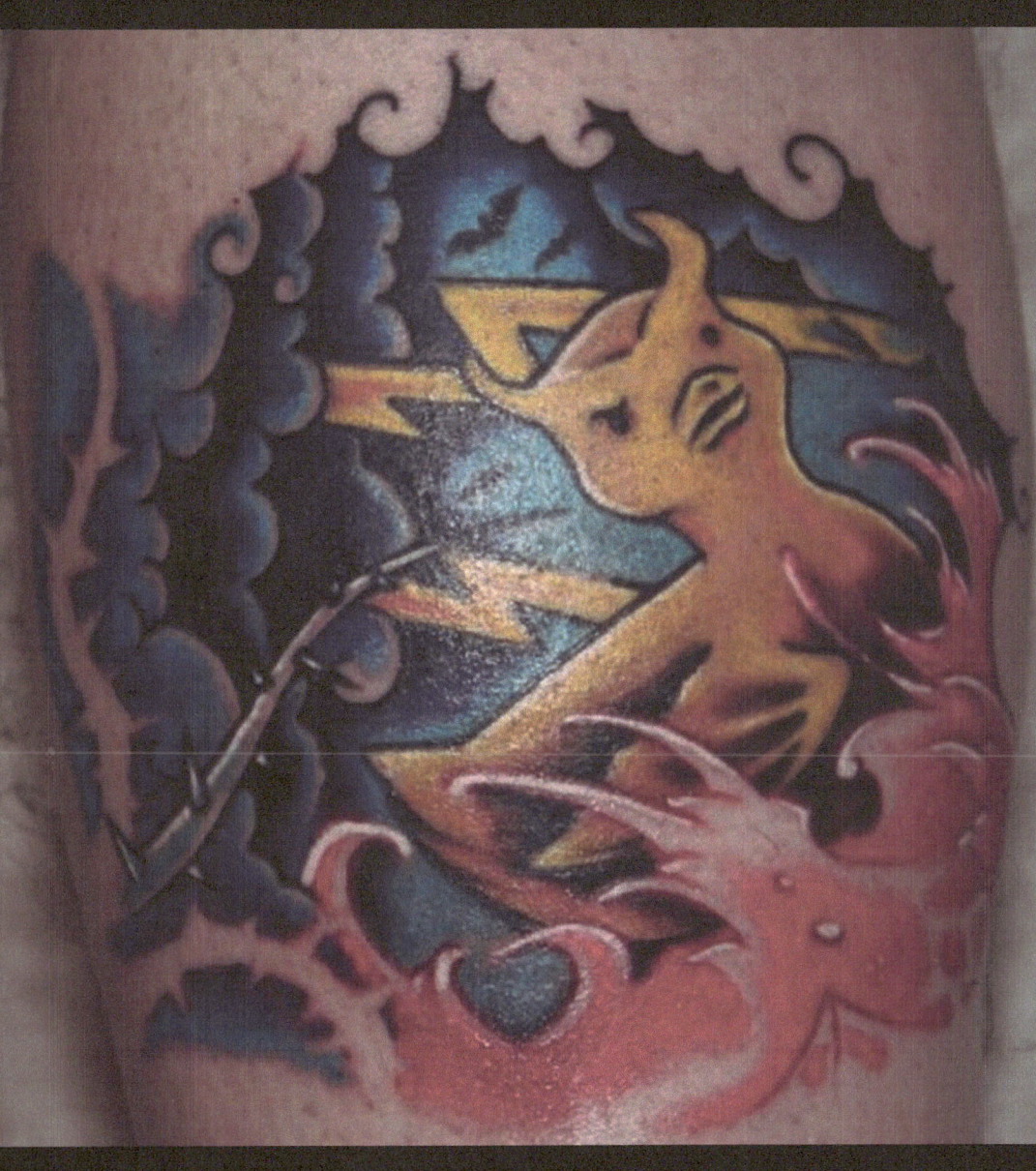

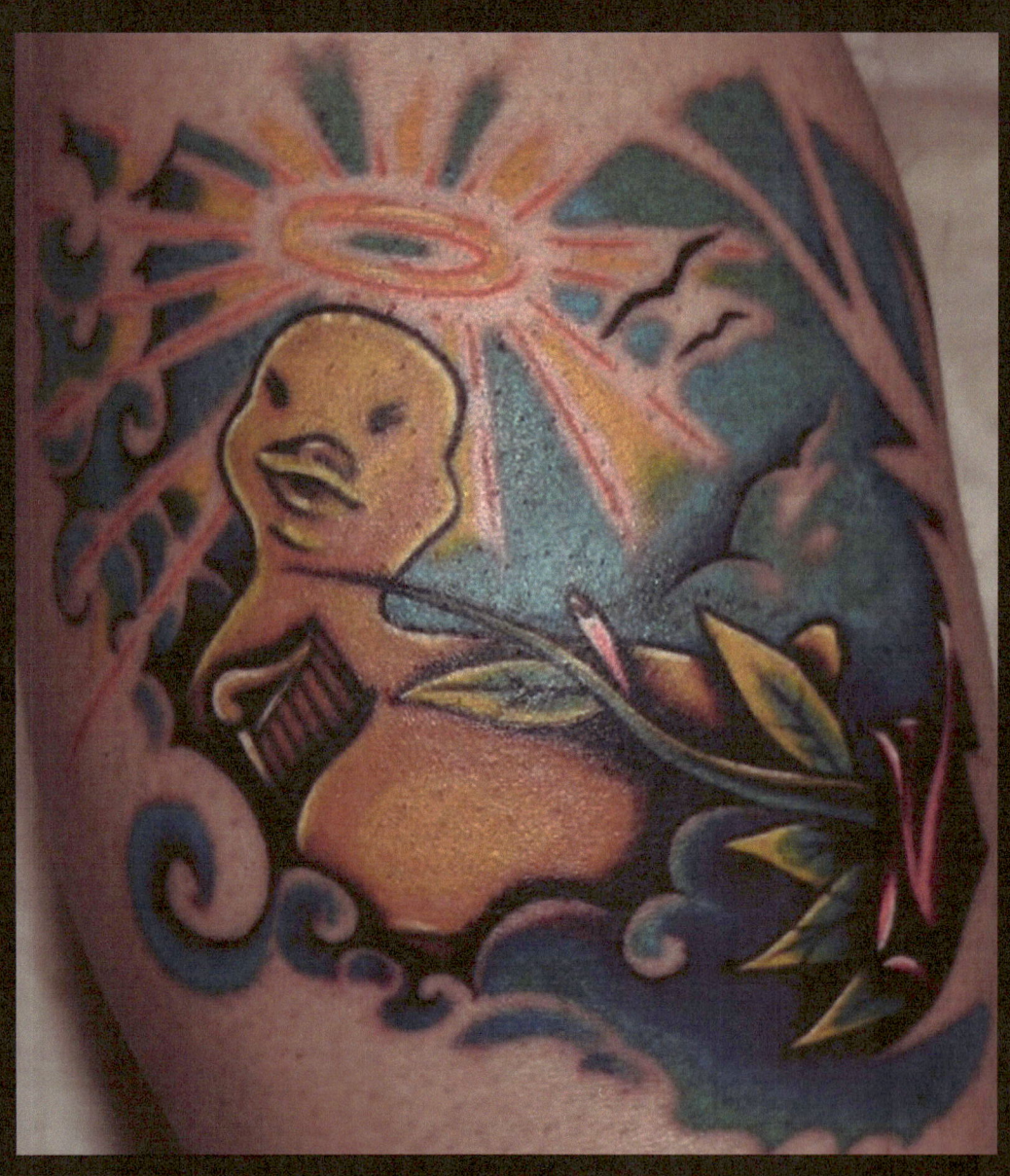

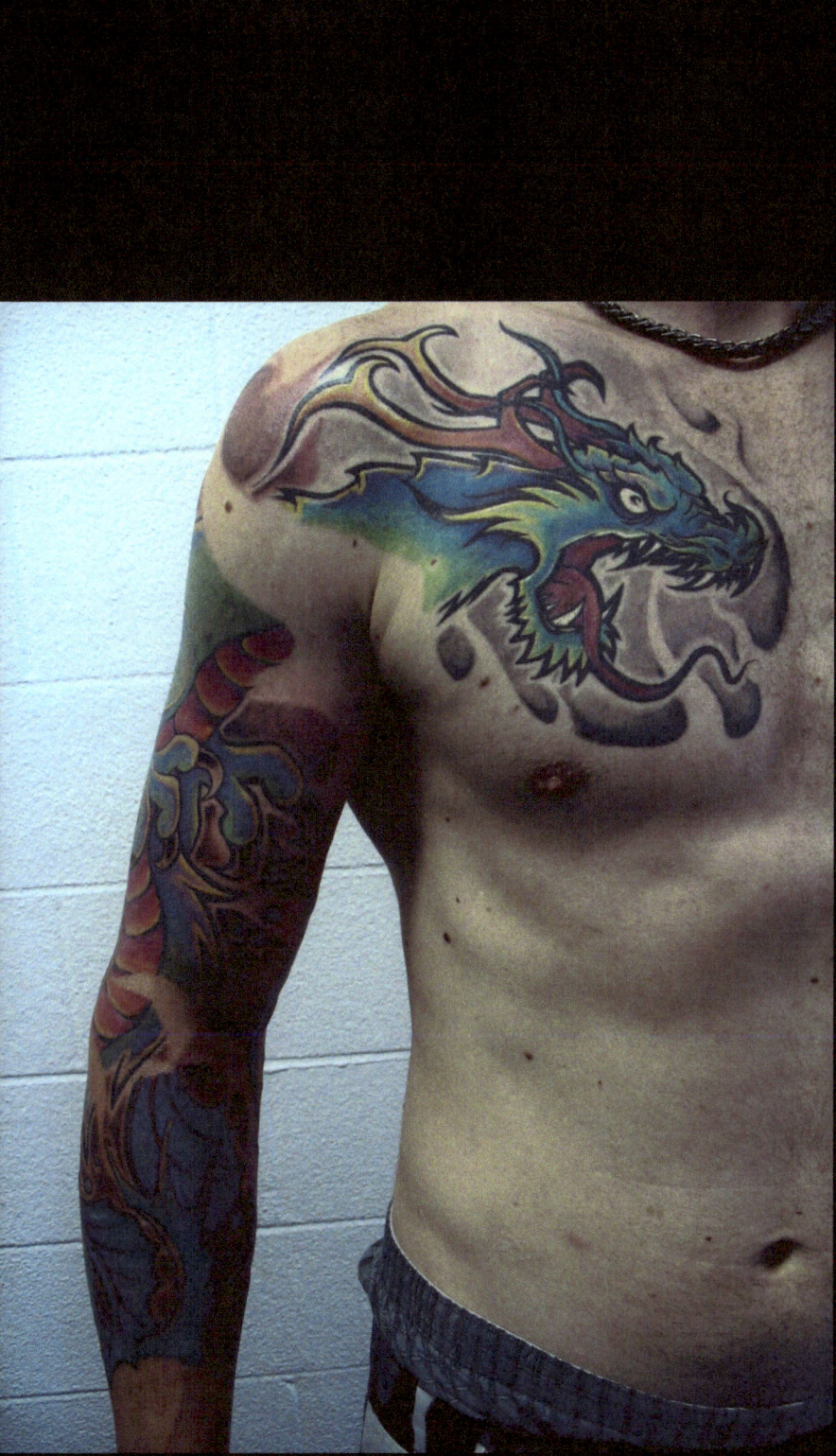

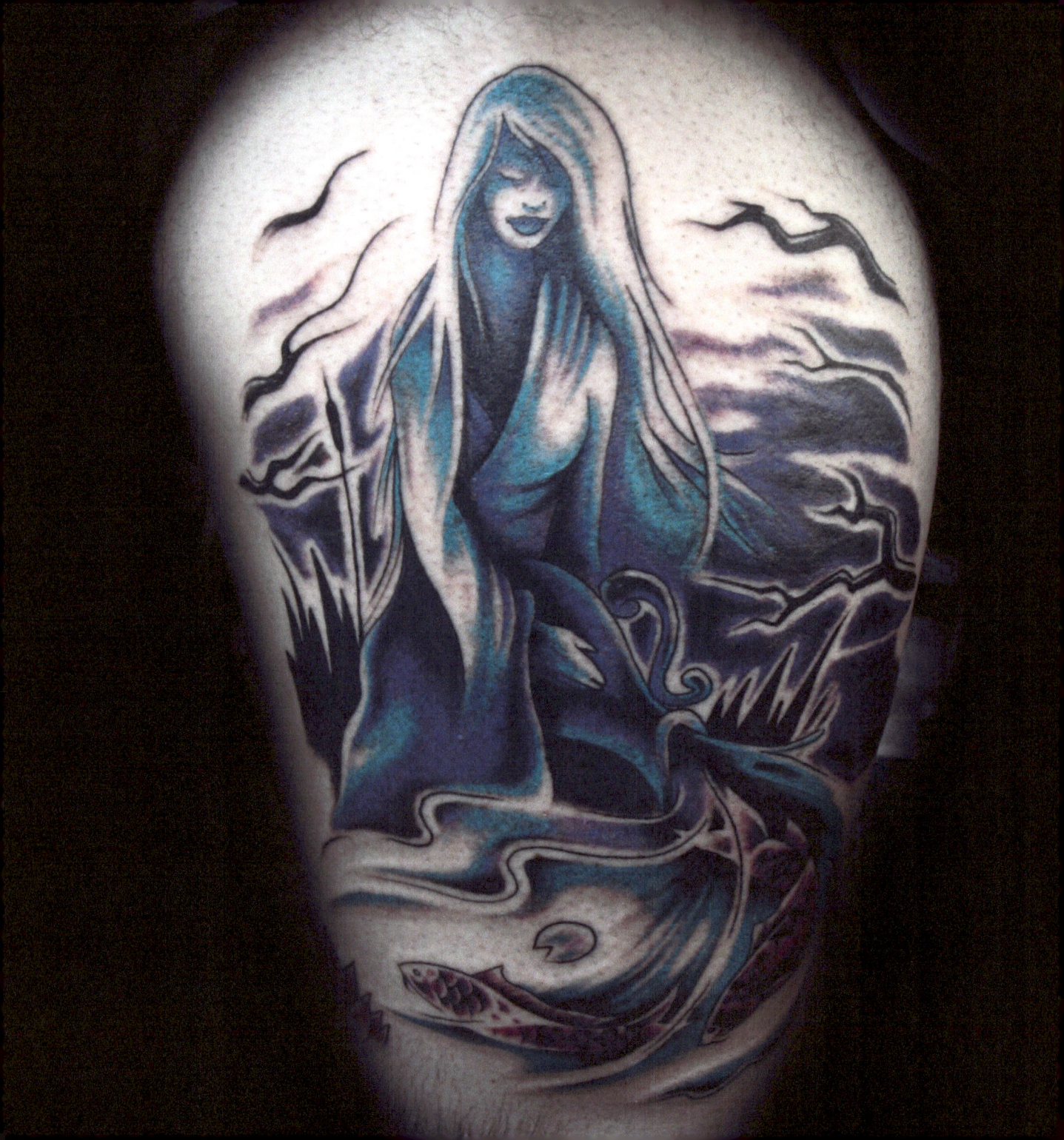

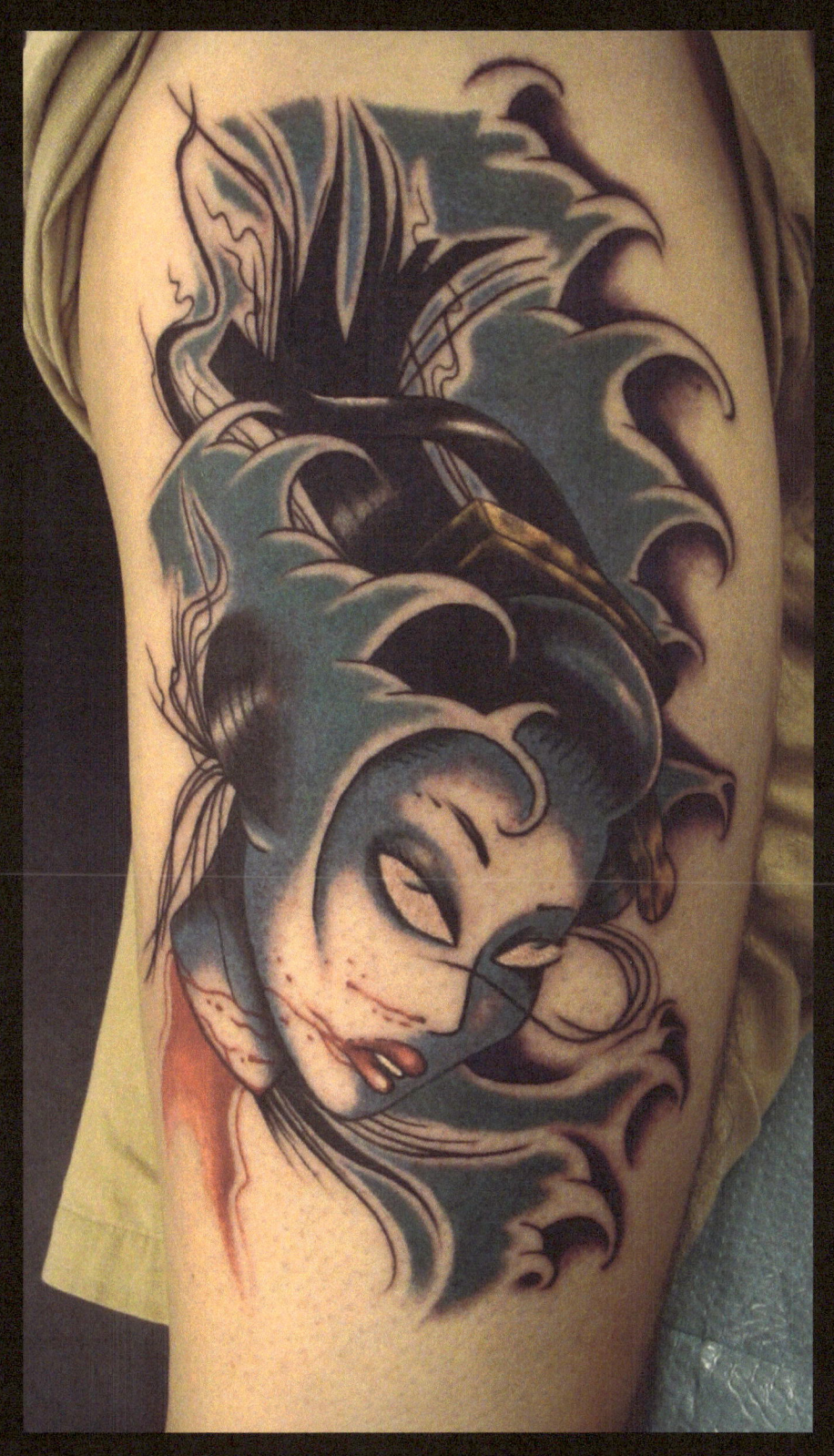

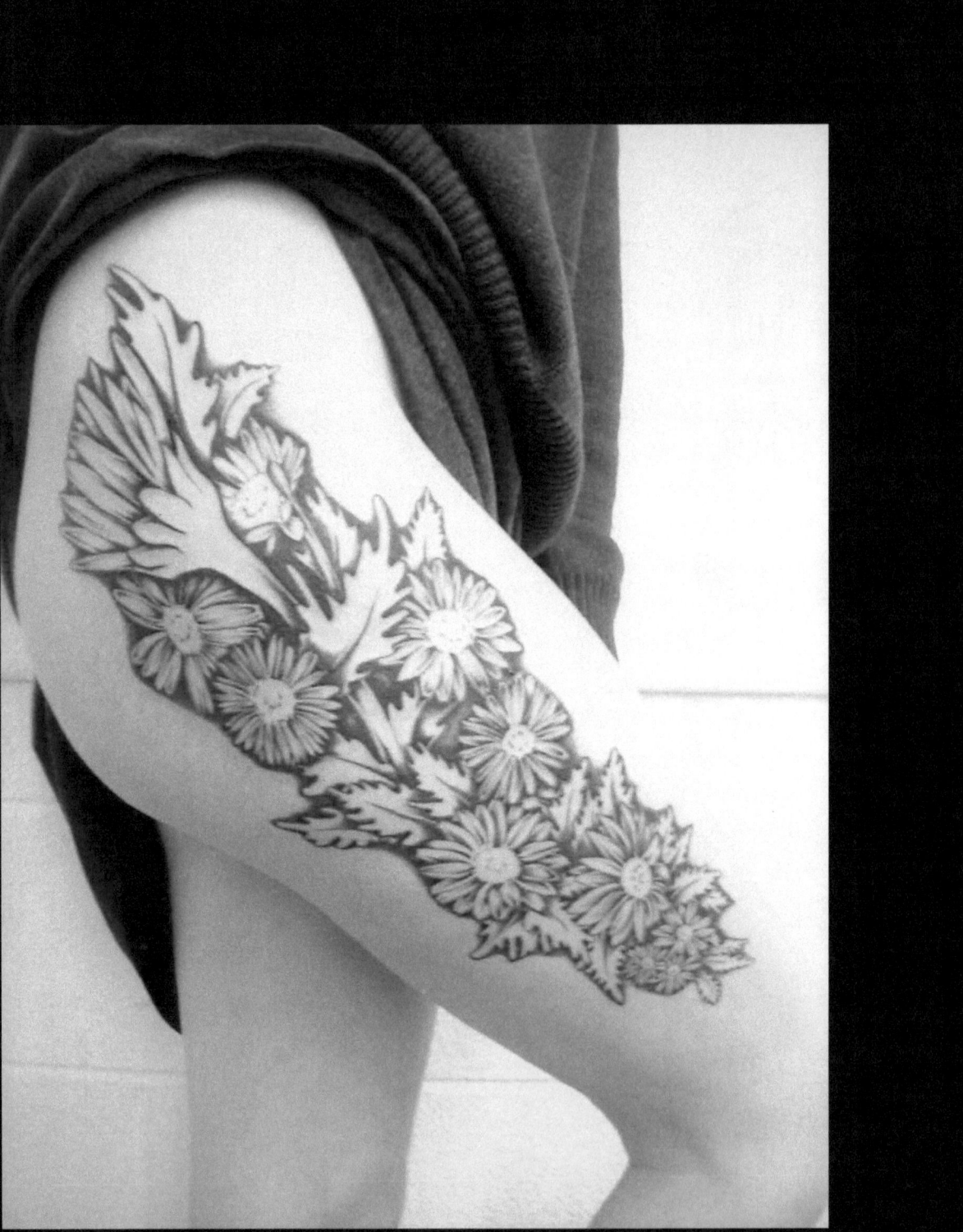

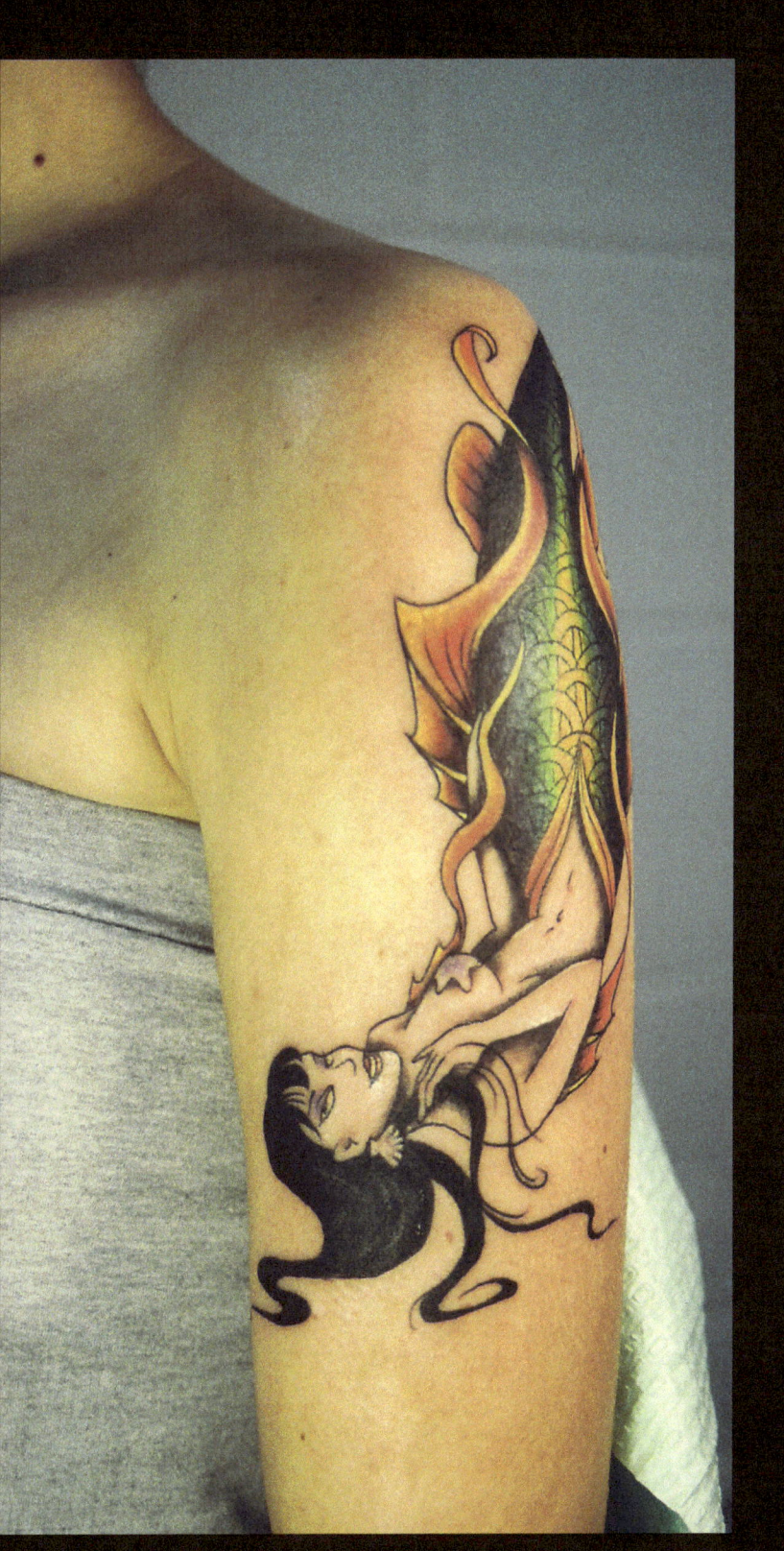

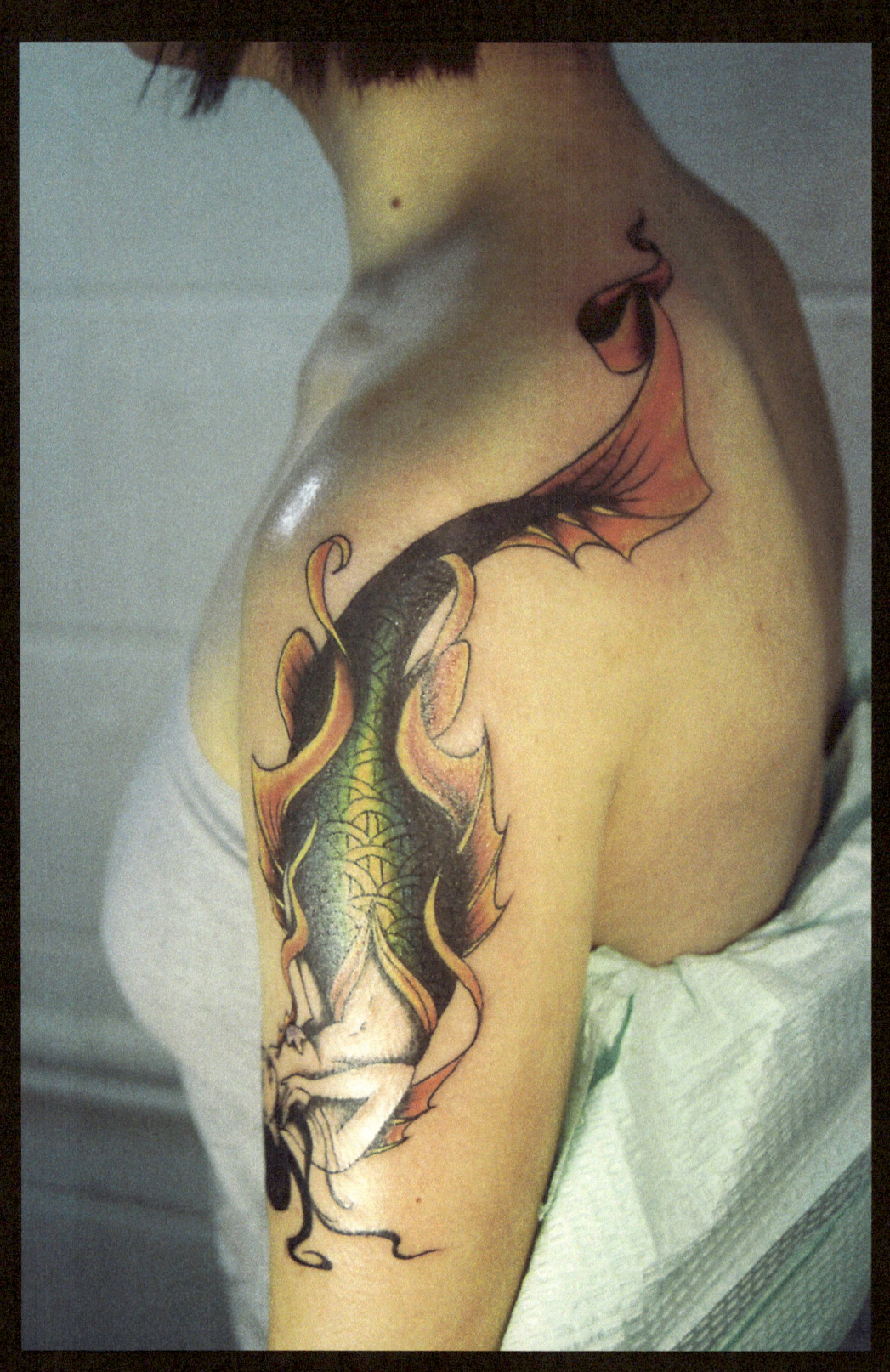

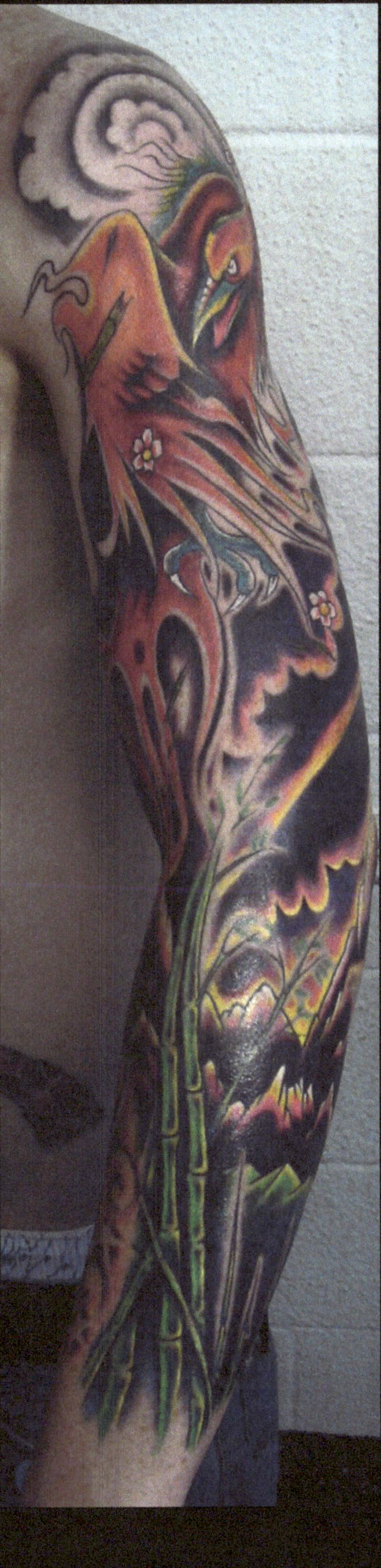
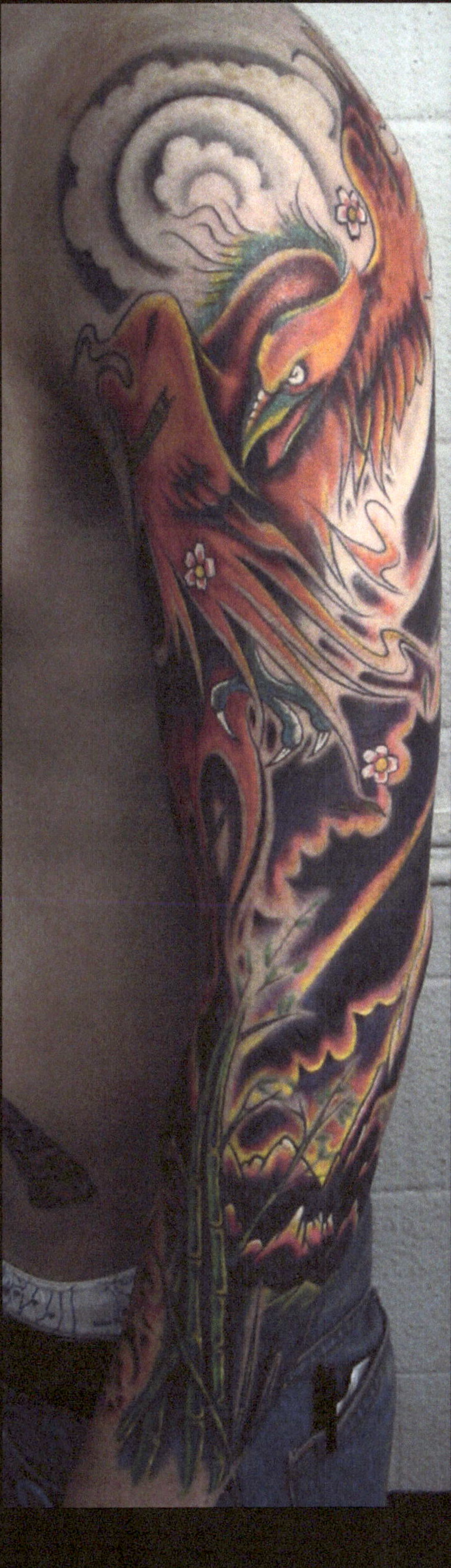

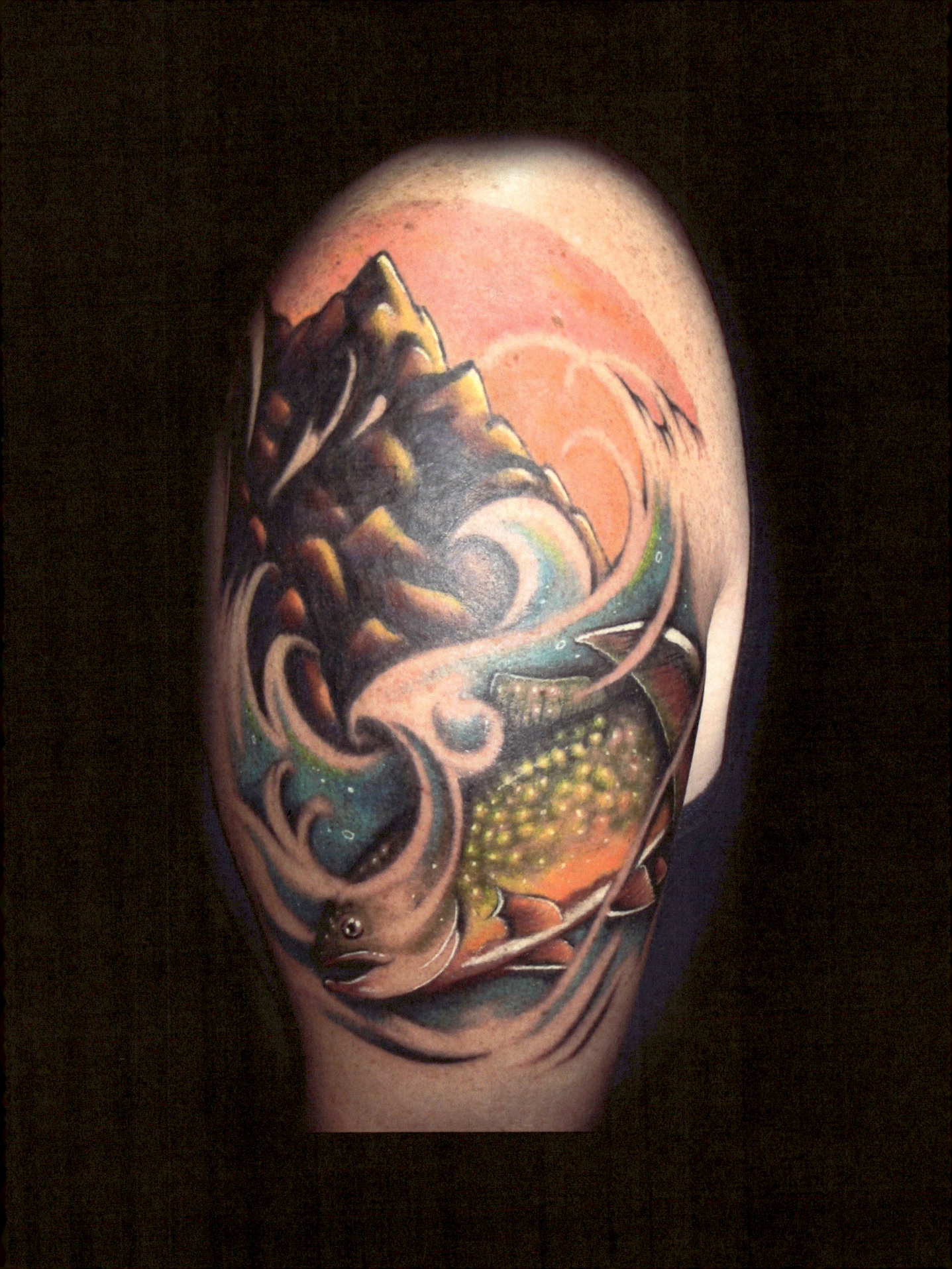

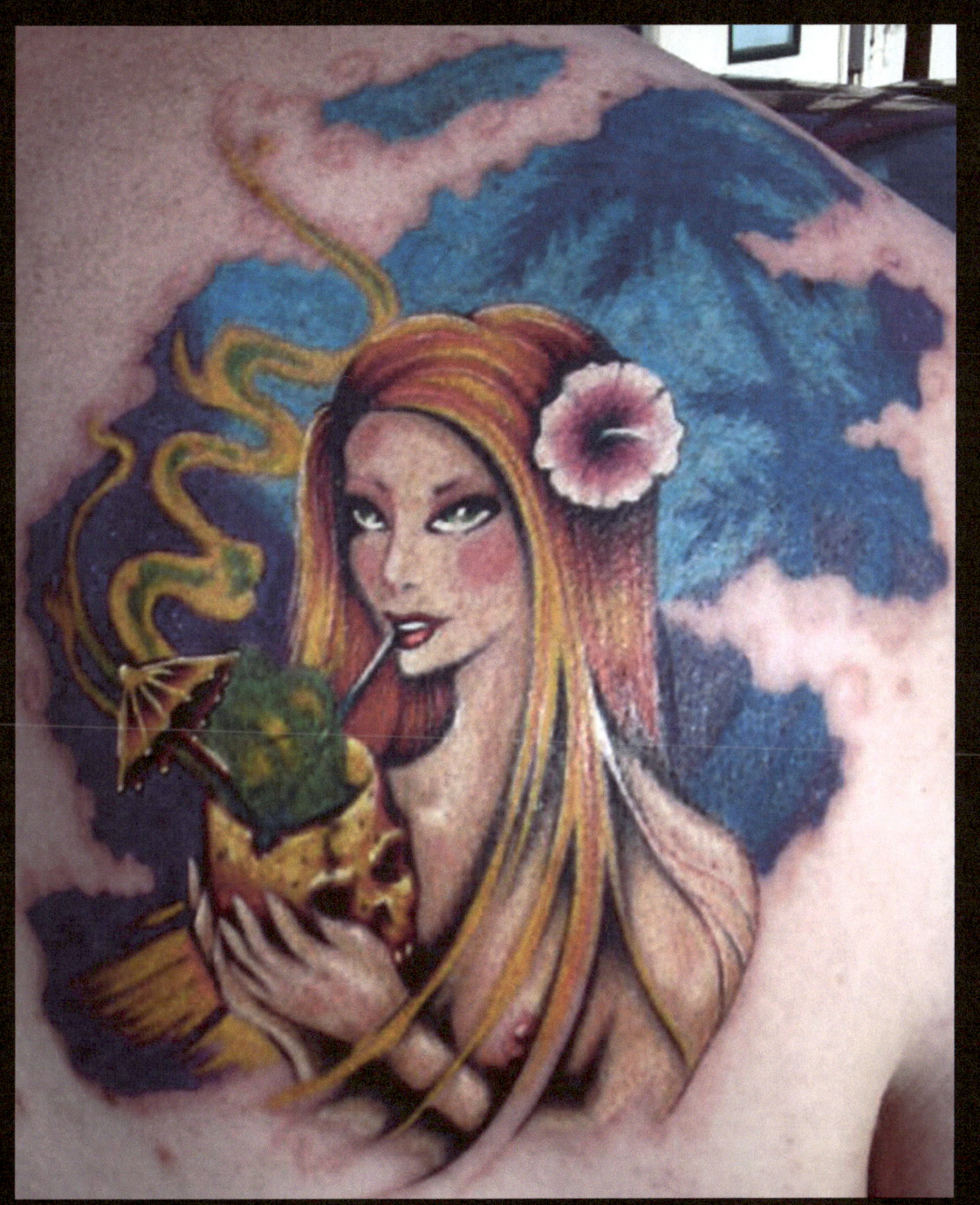

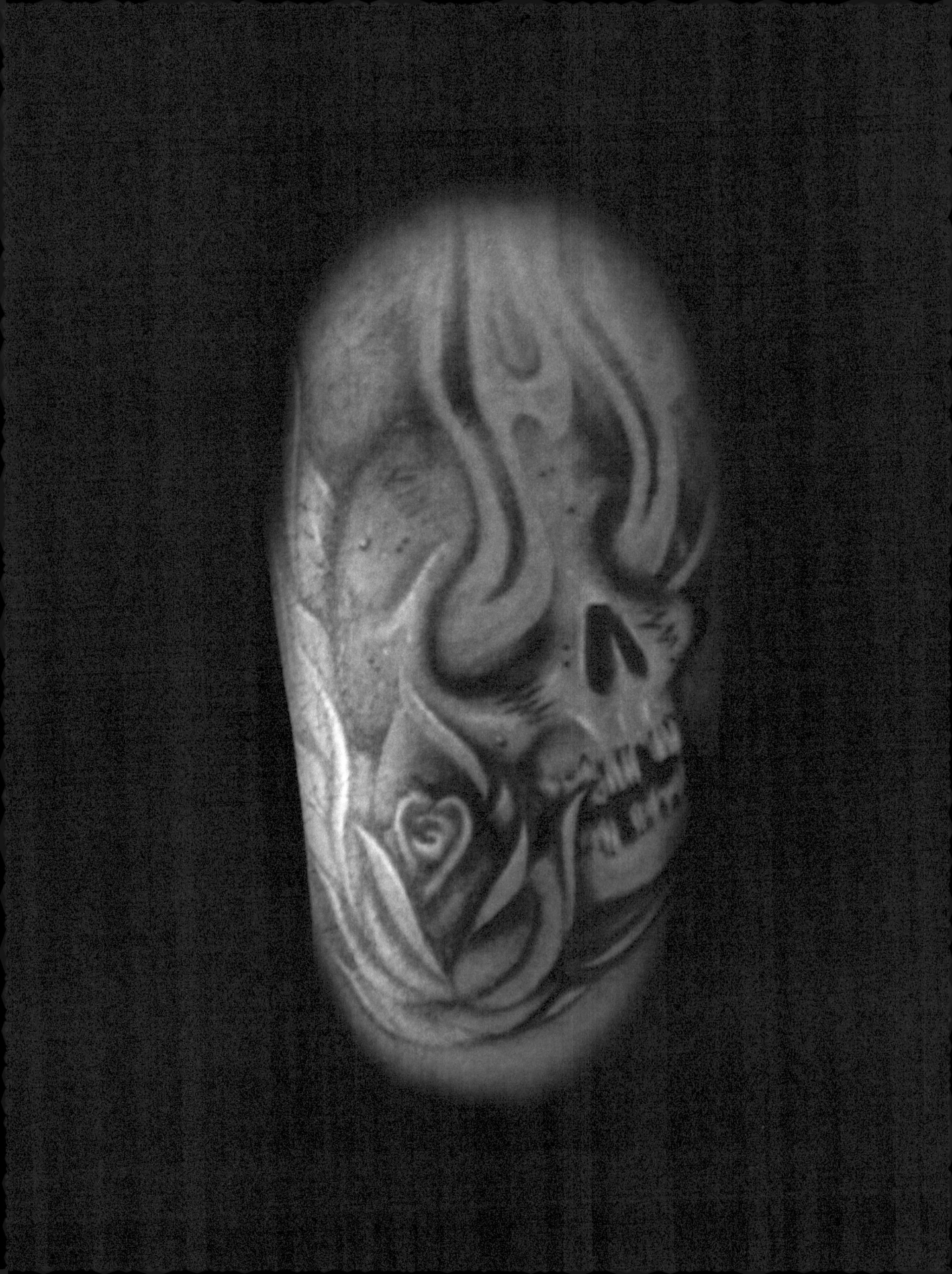

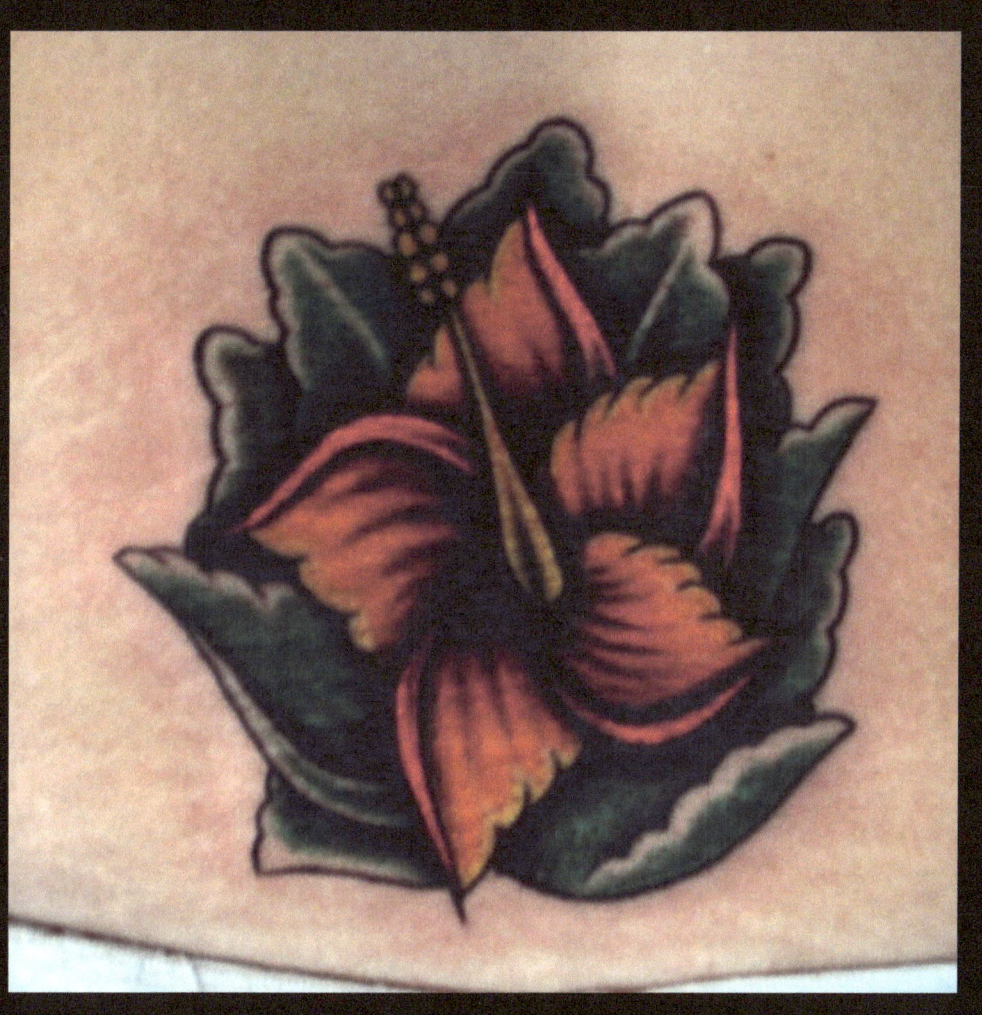

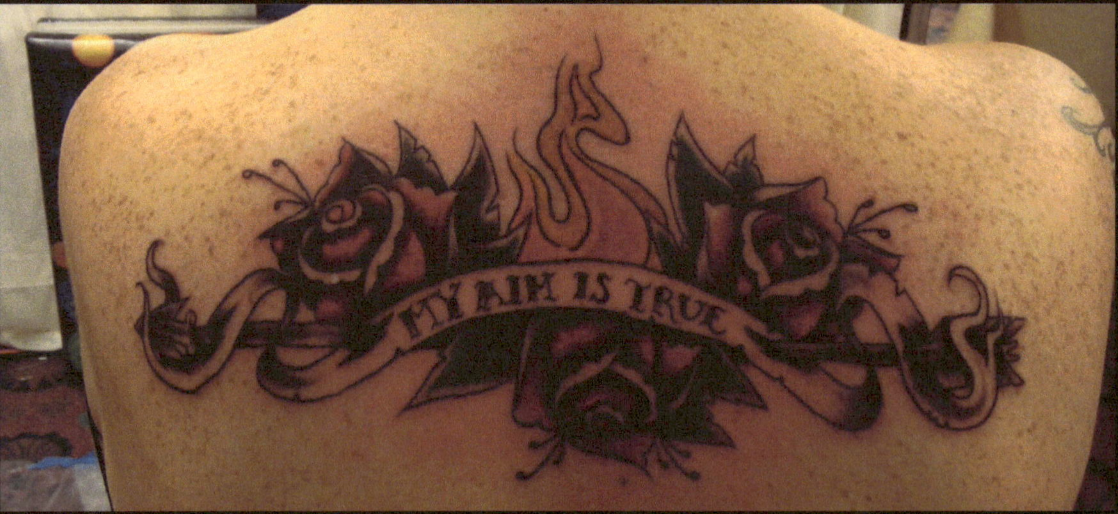
MY AIM IS TRUE

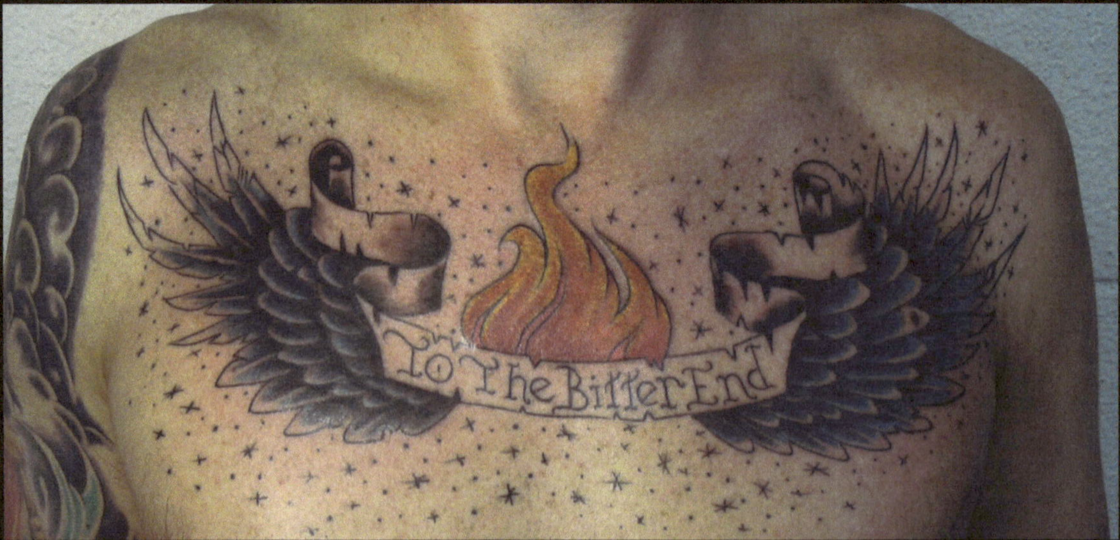
To The Bitter End

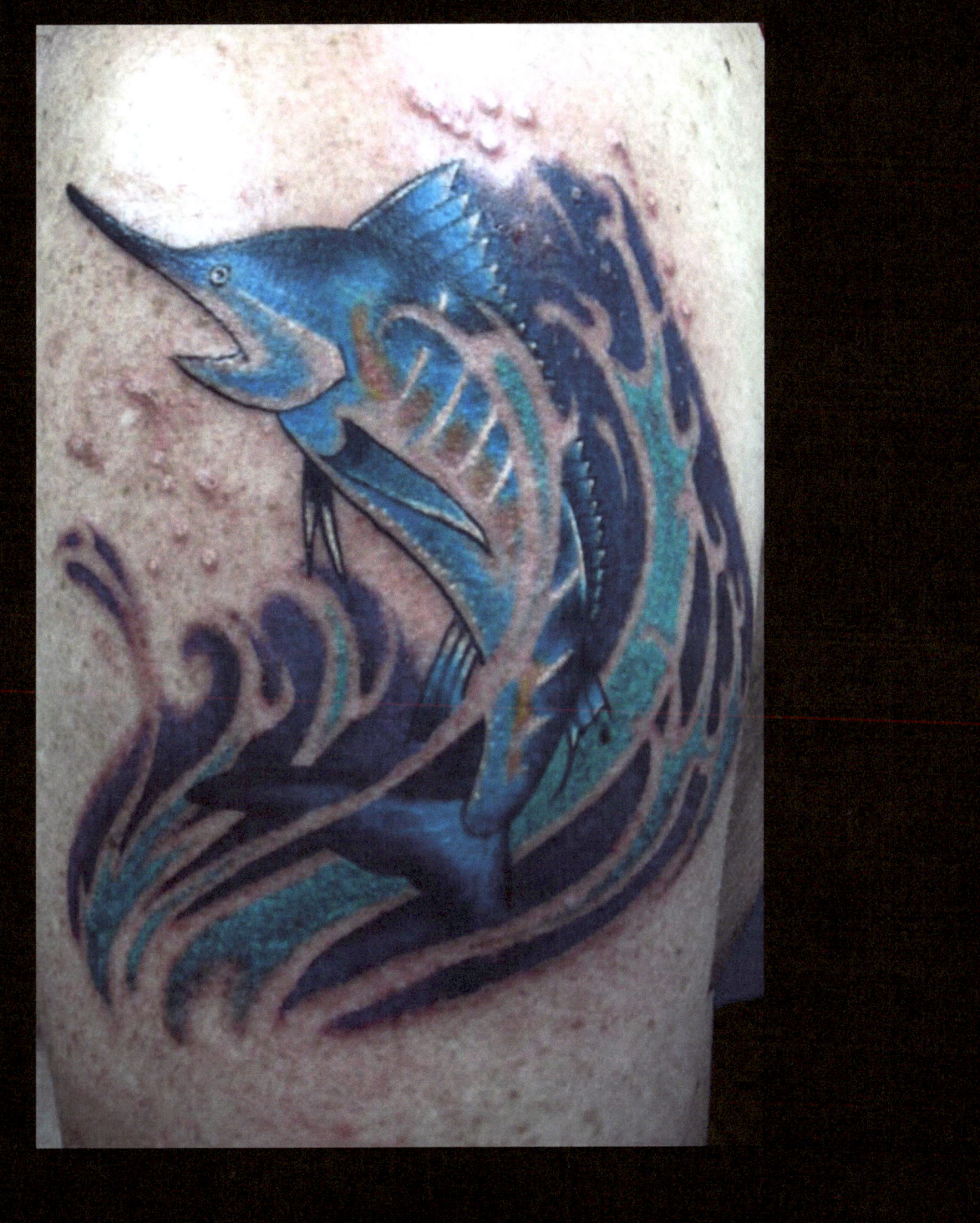

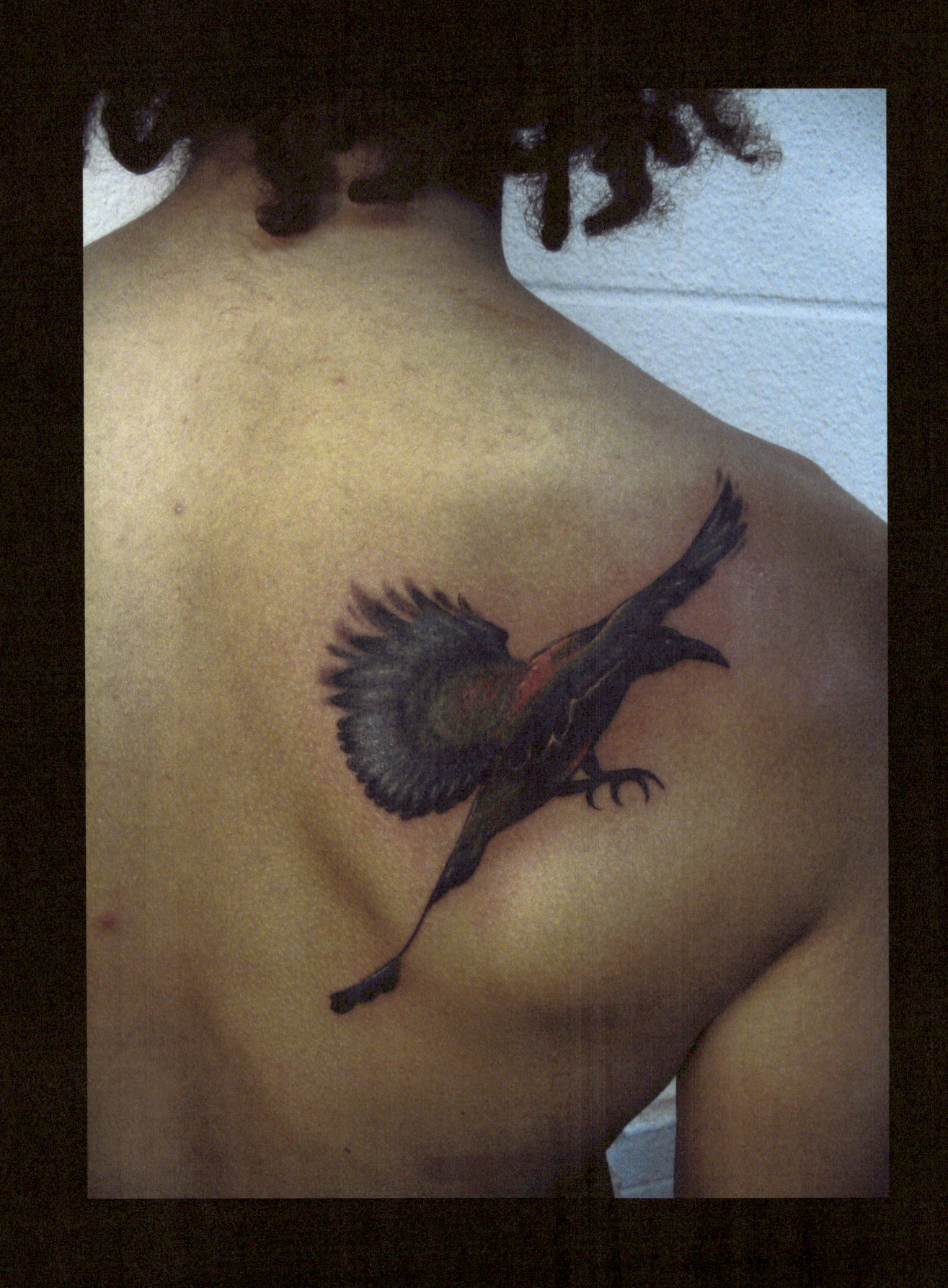

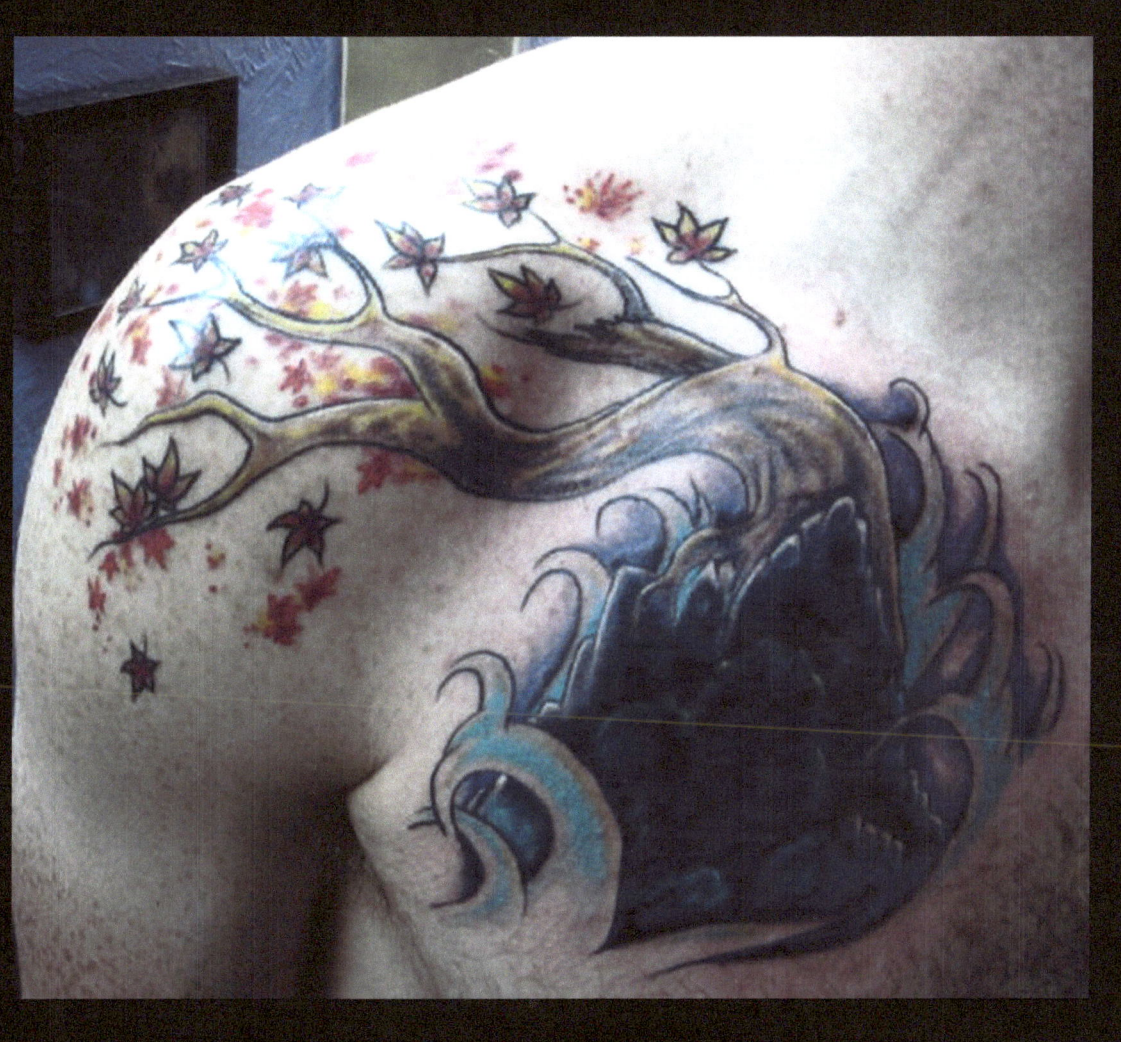

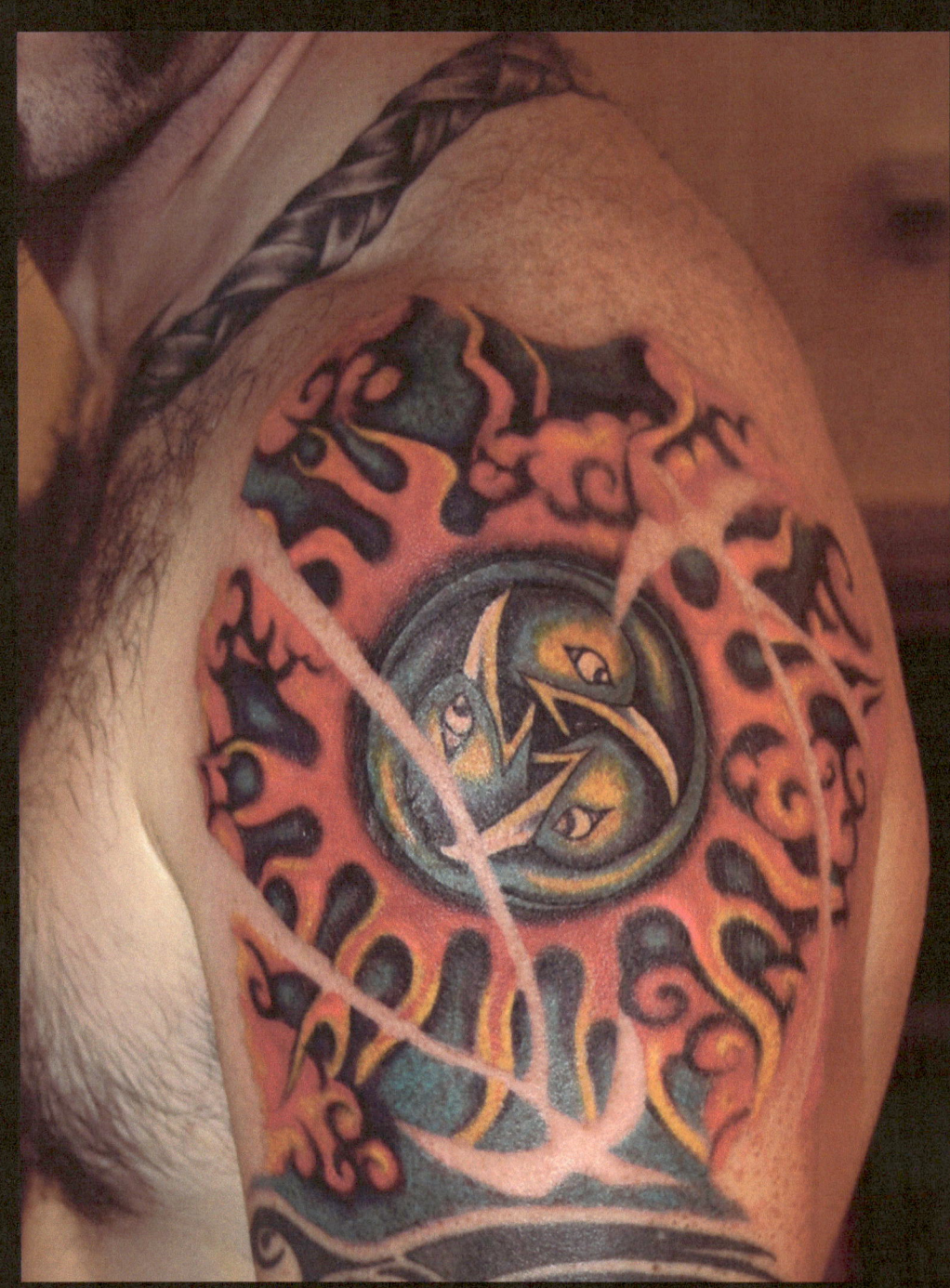

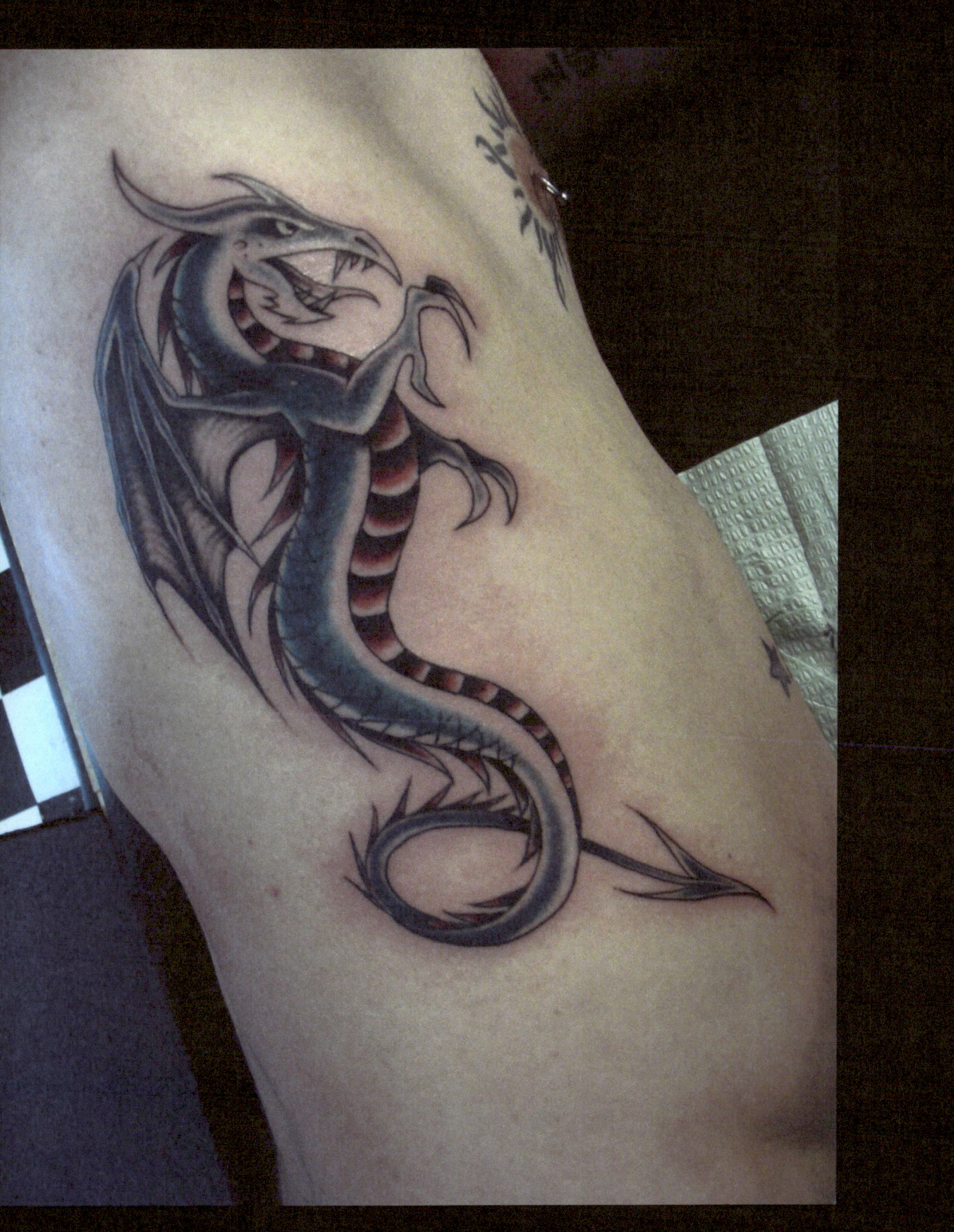

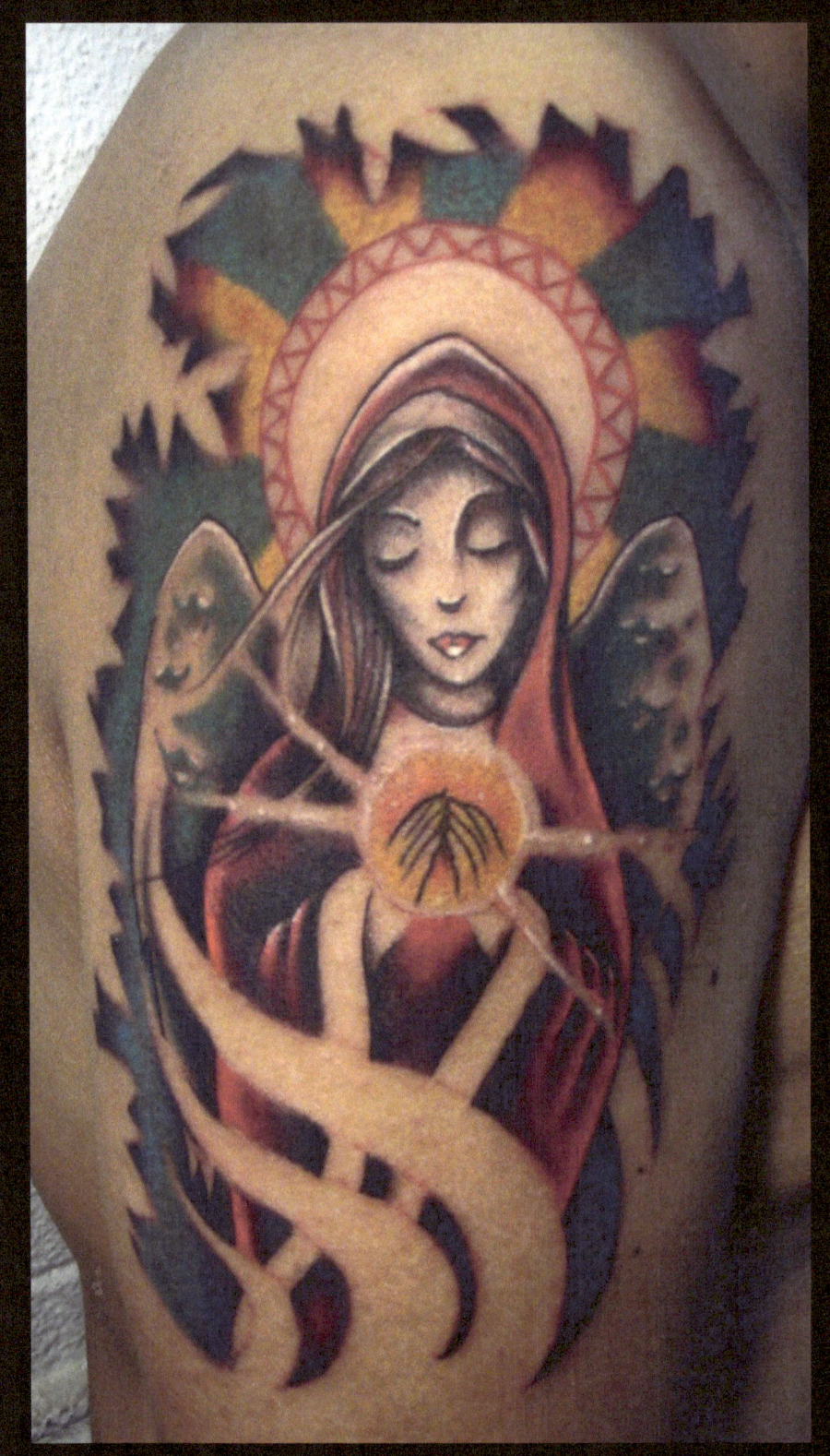

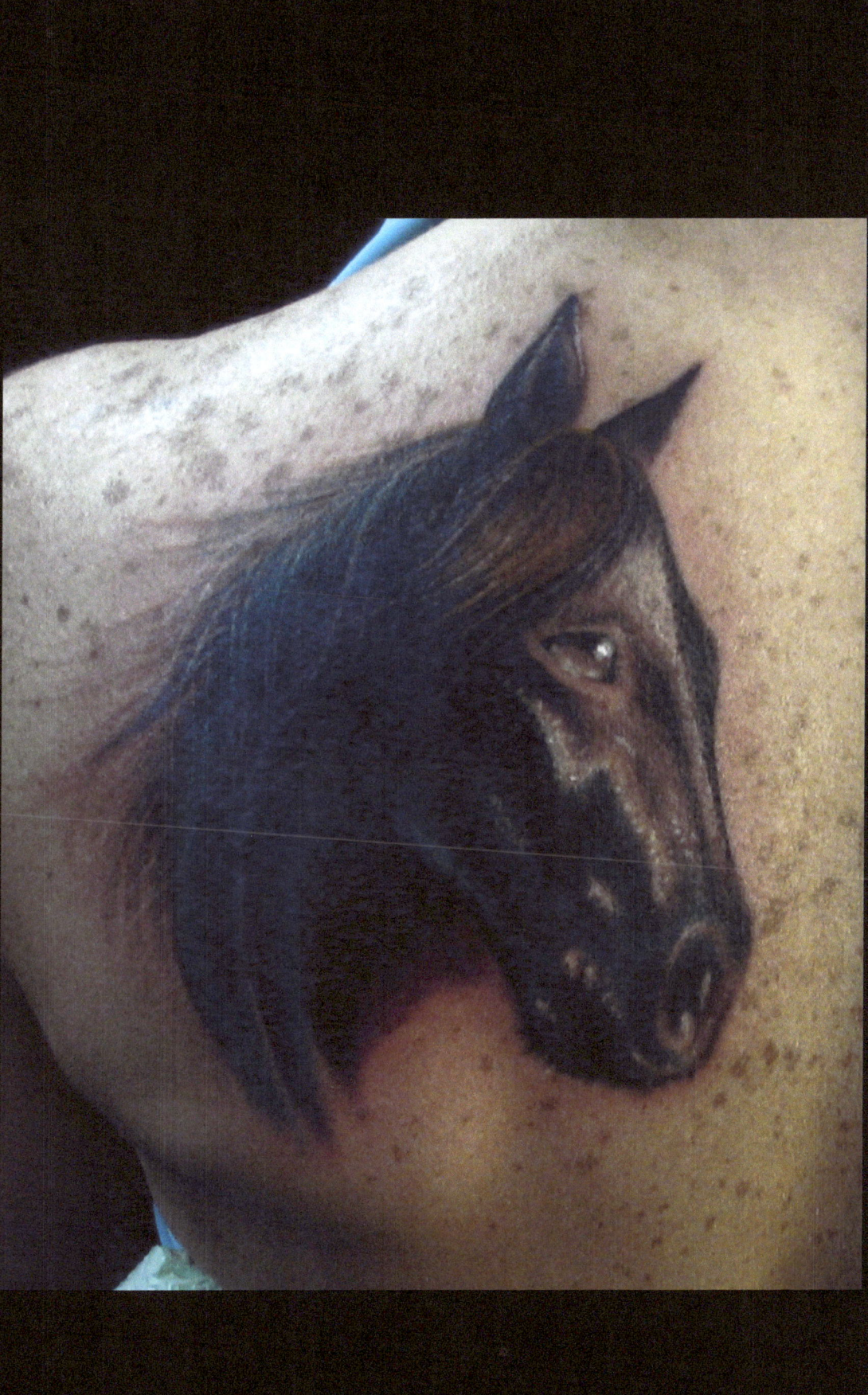

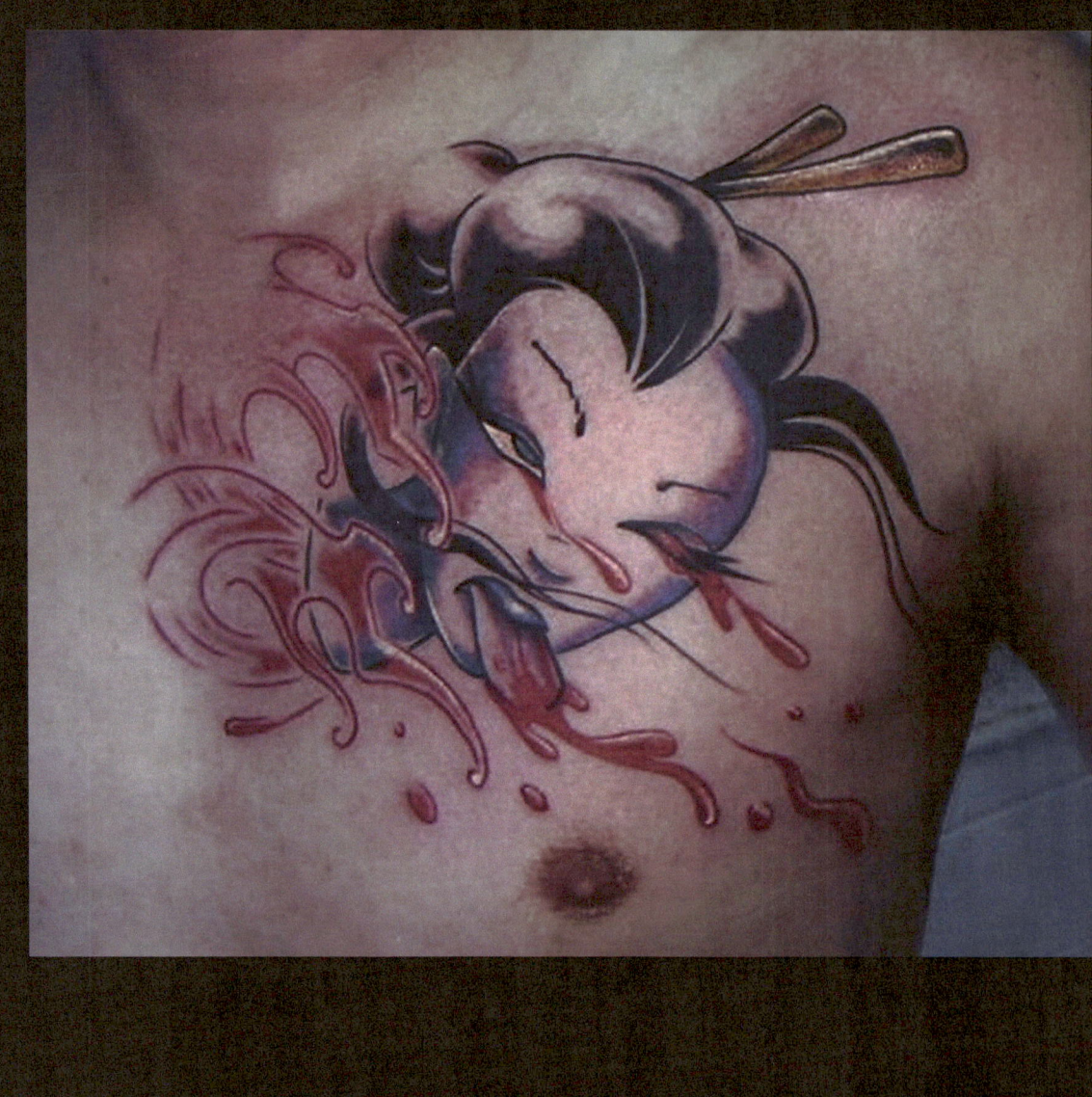

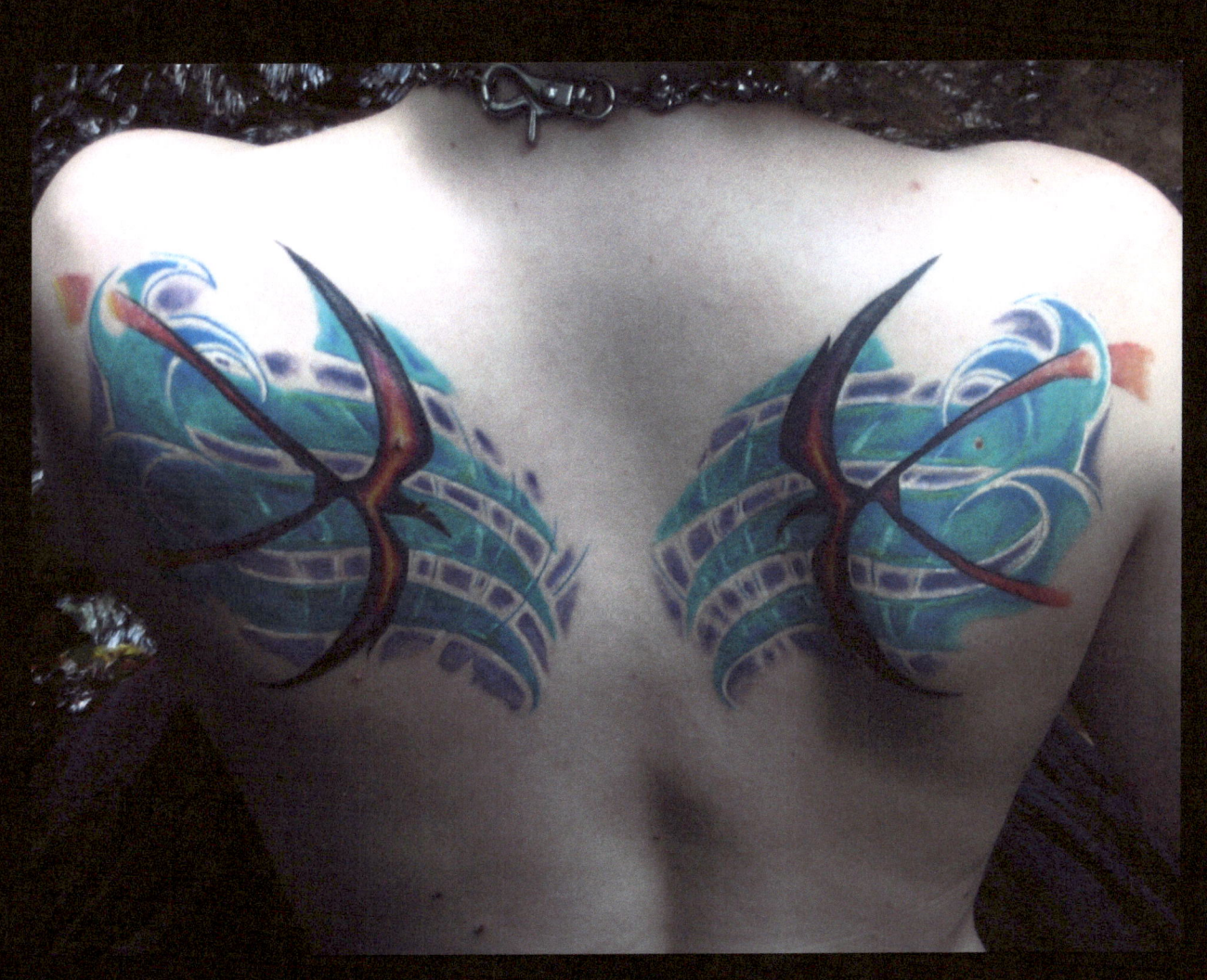

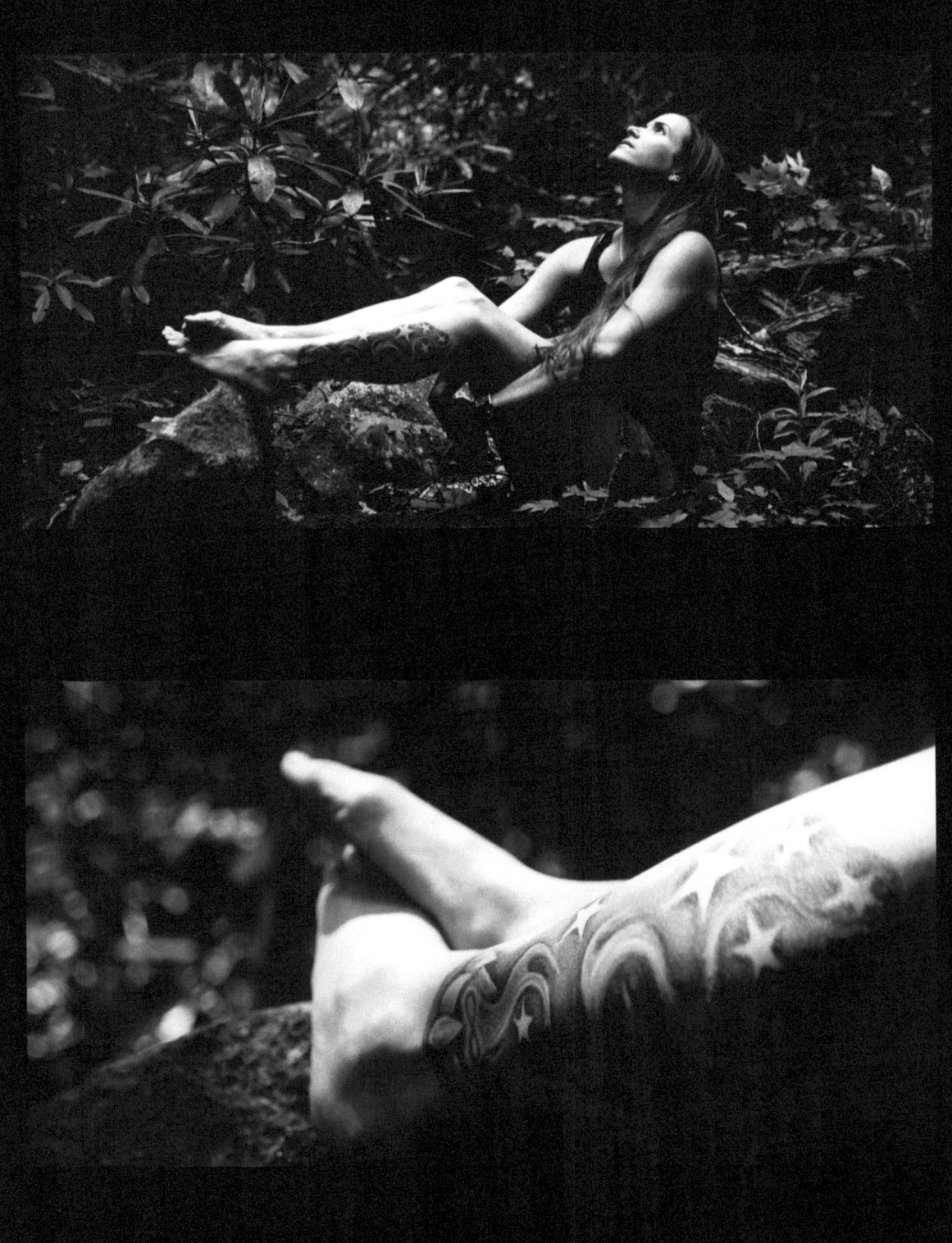

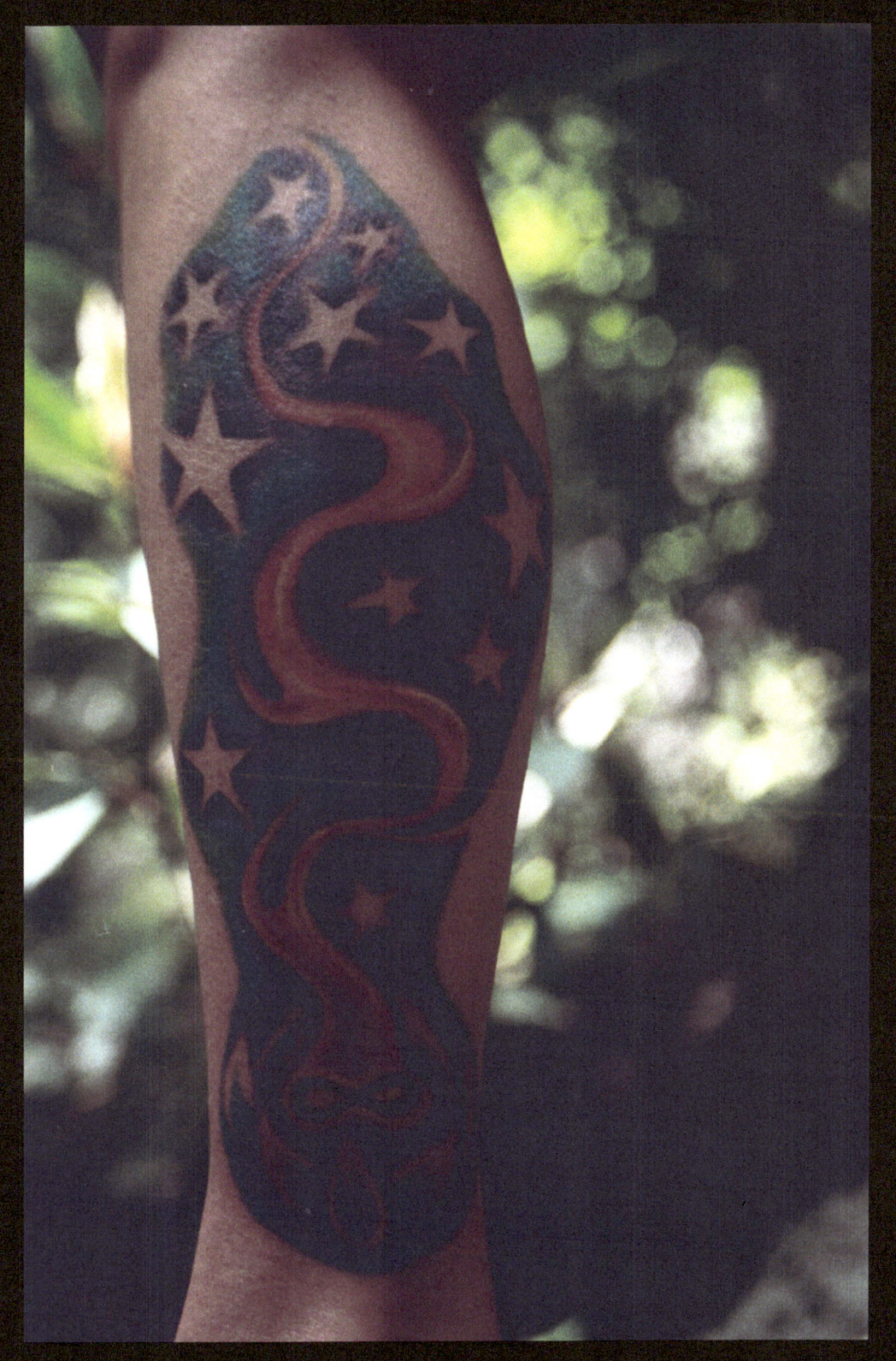

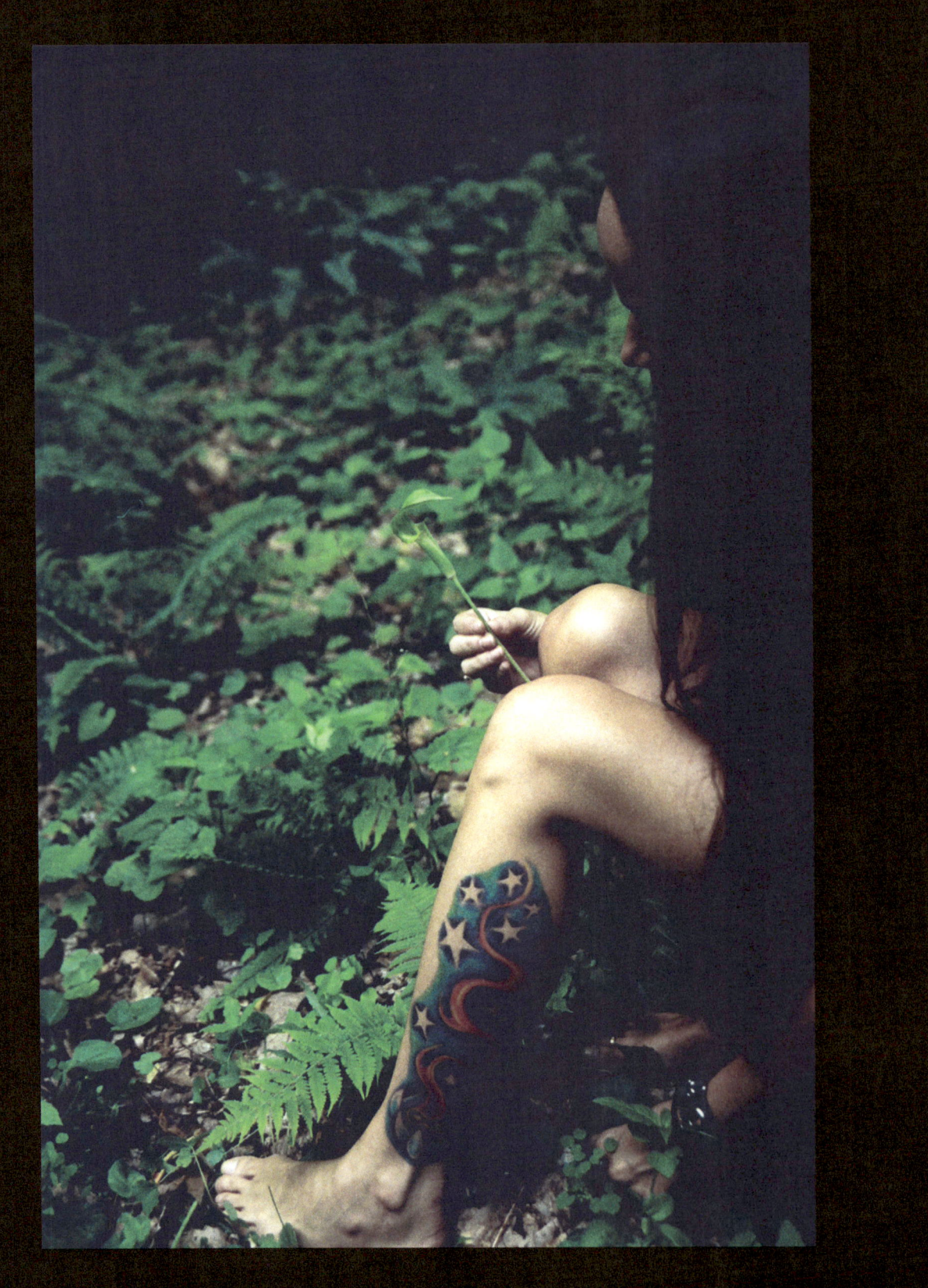

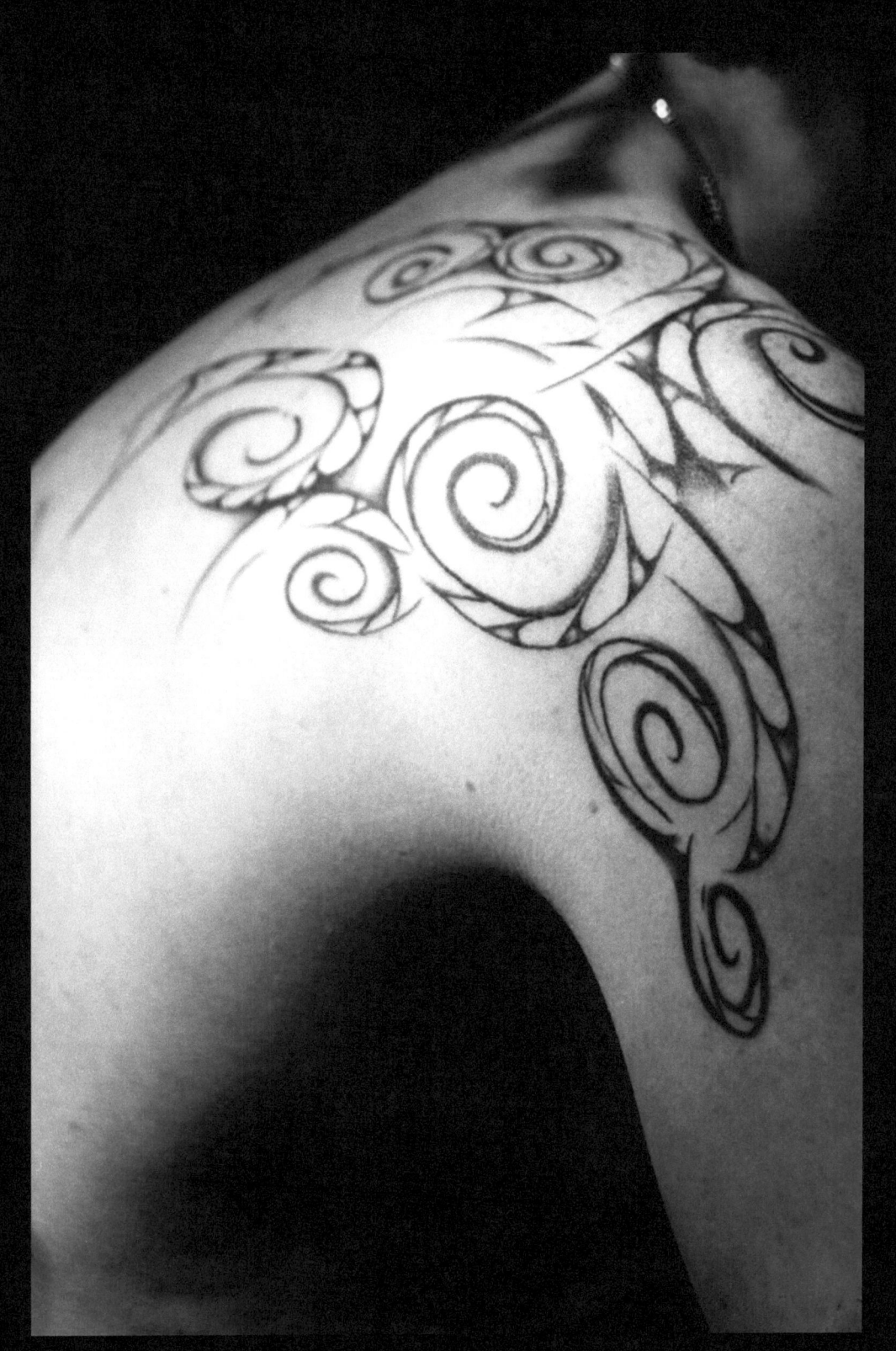

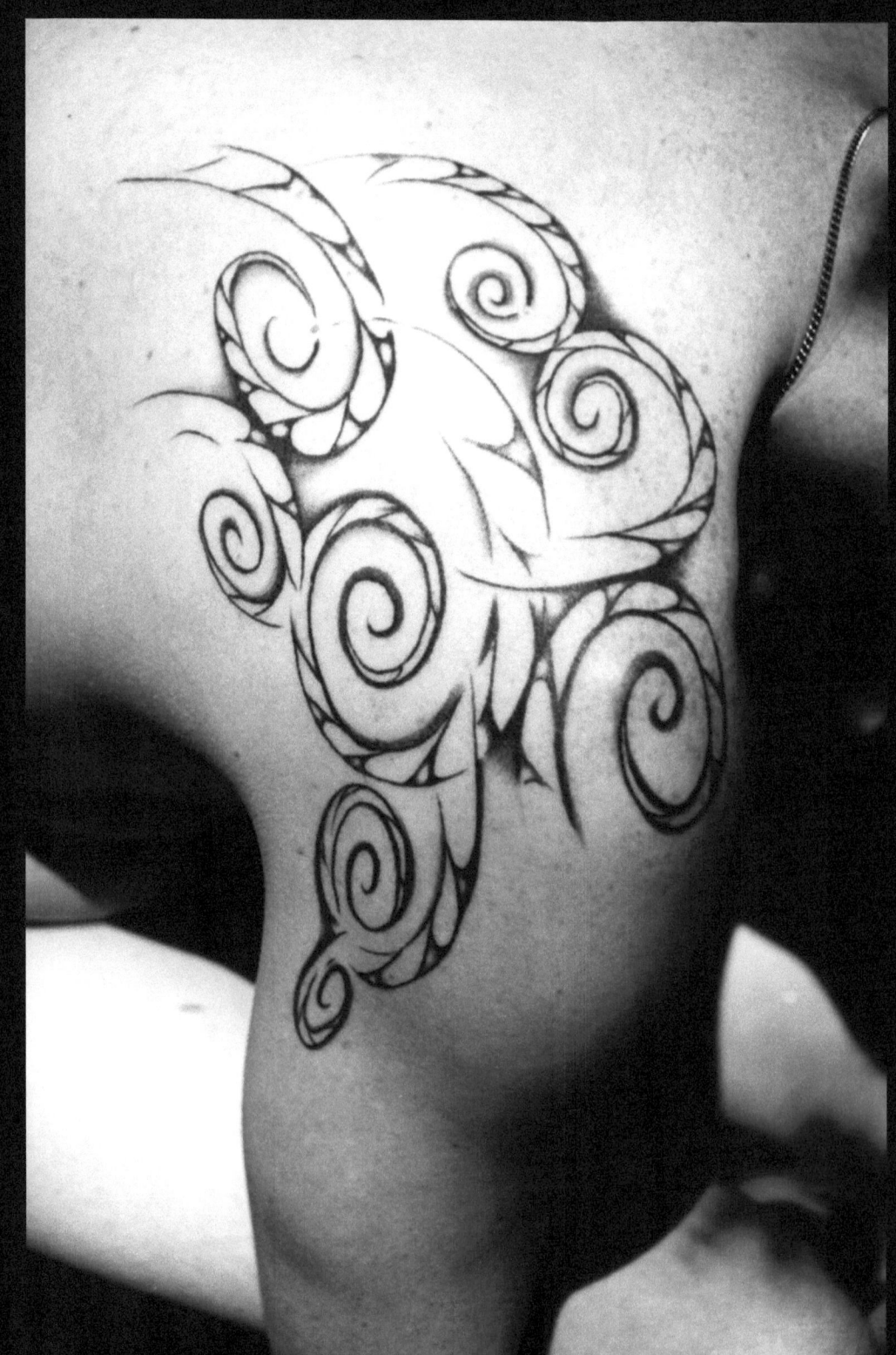

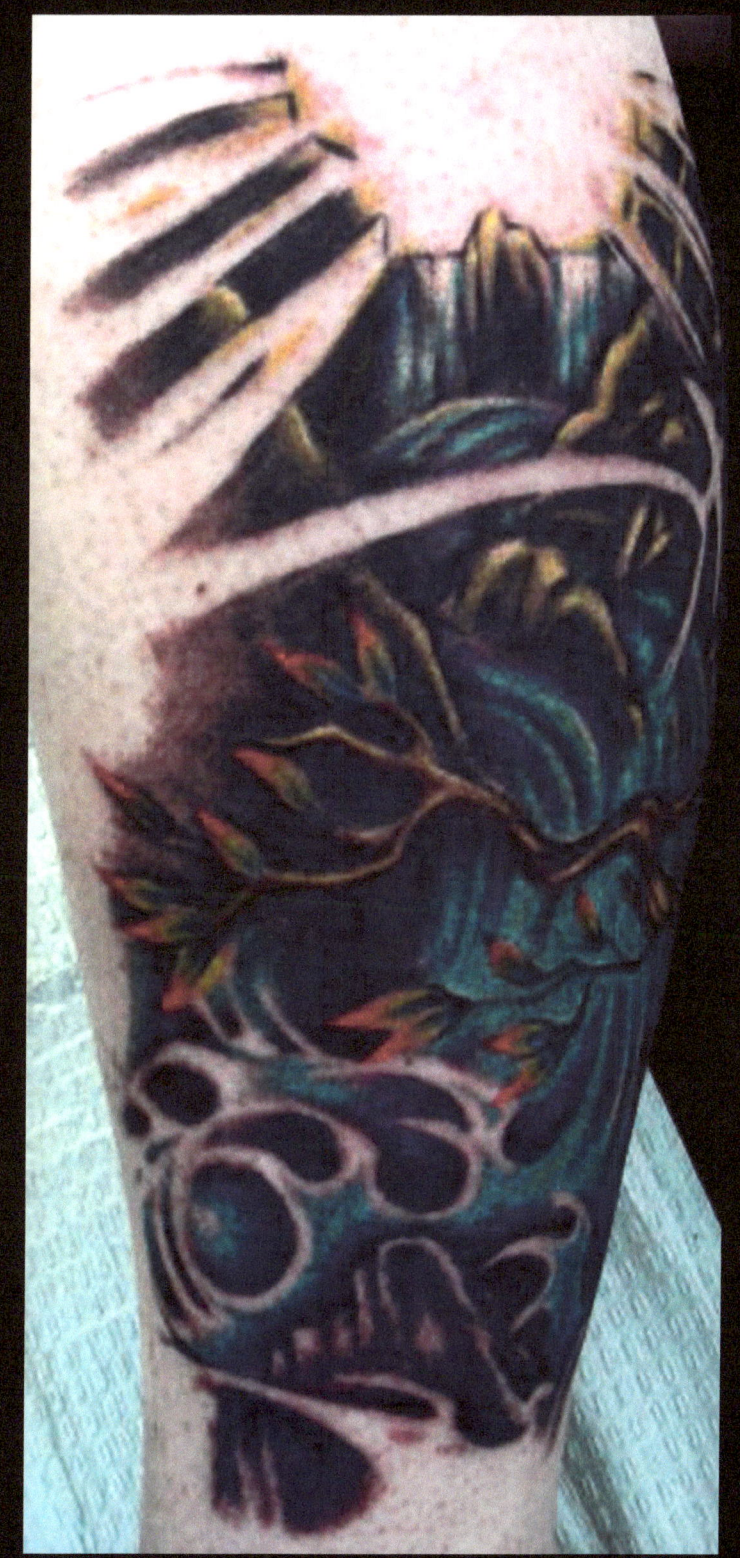

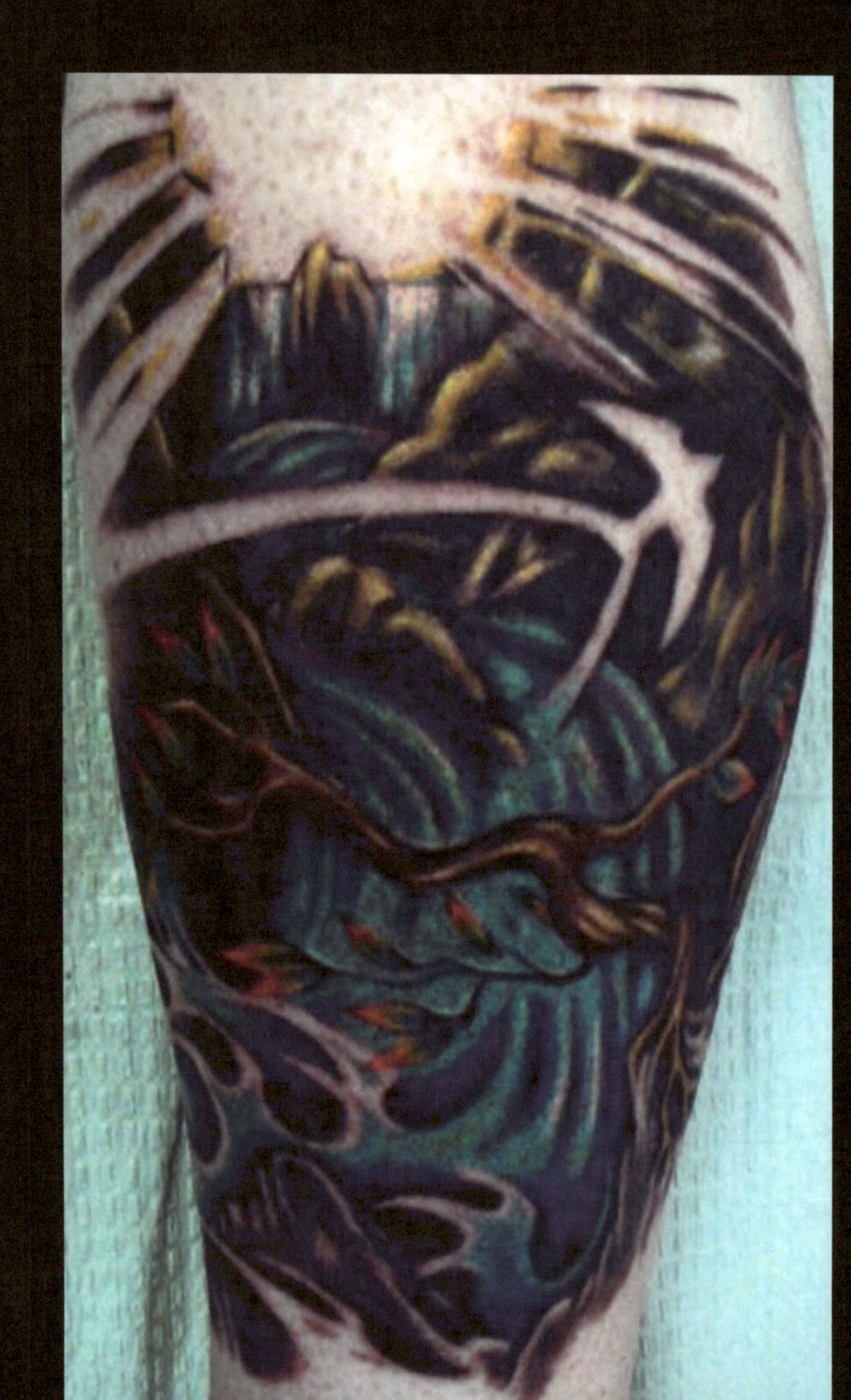

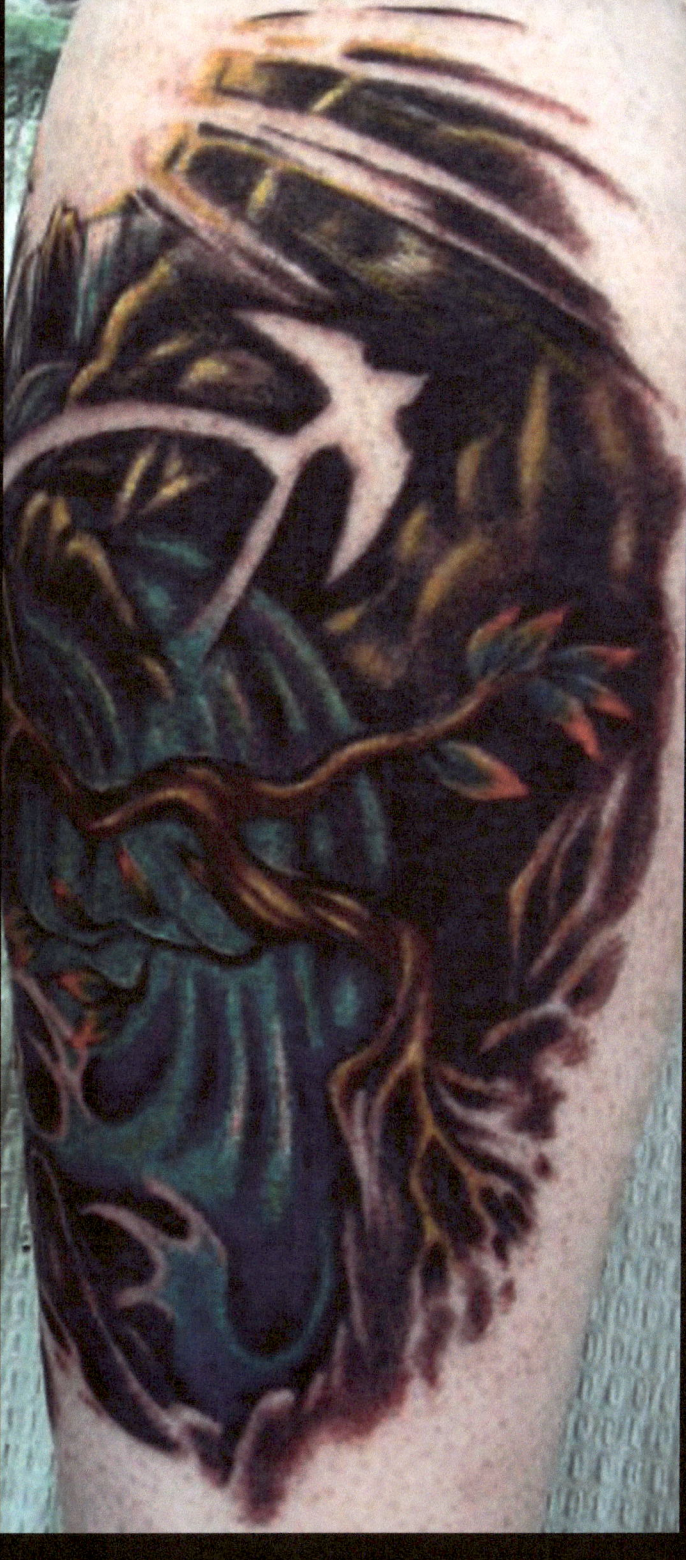

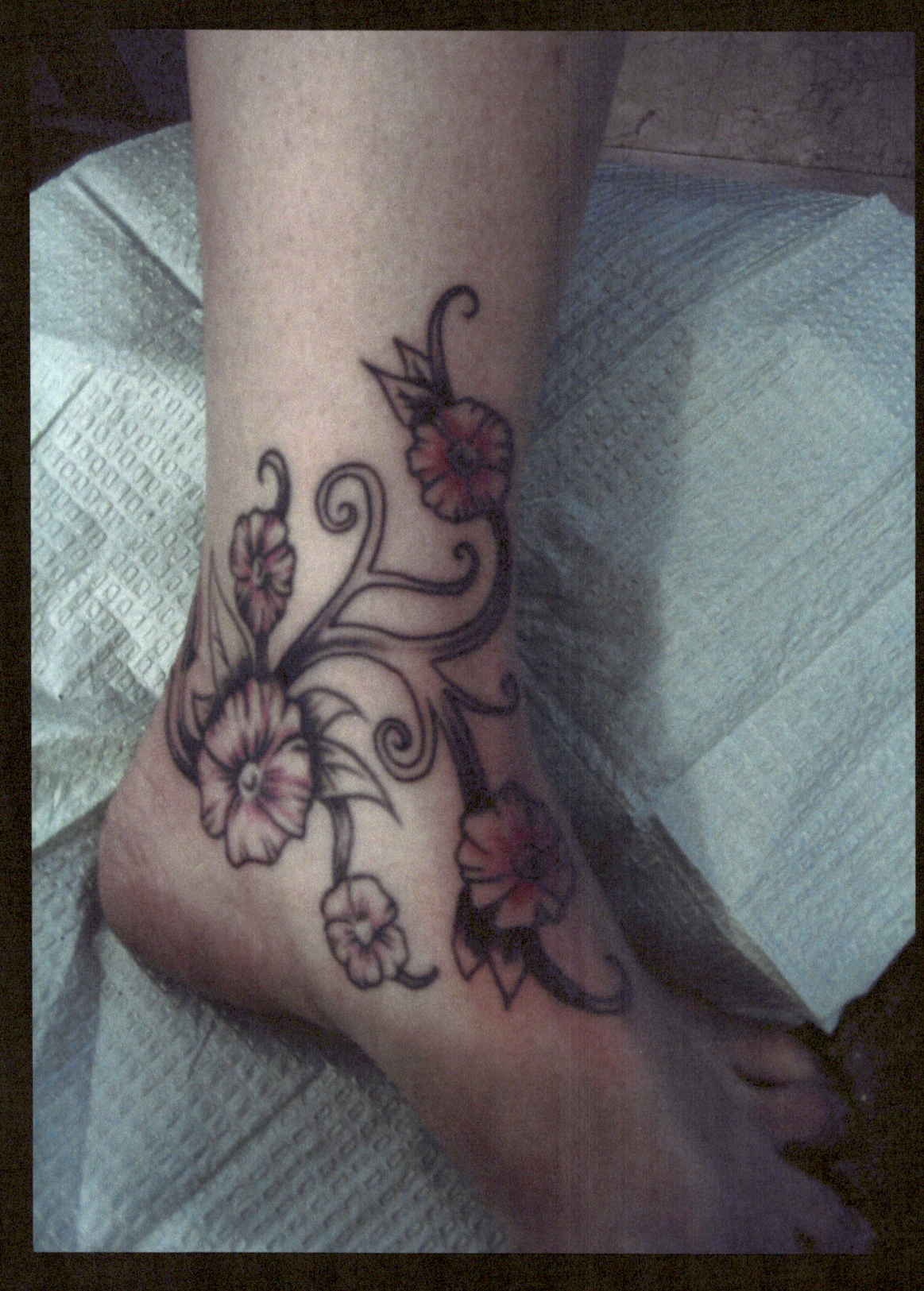

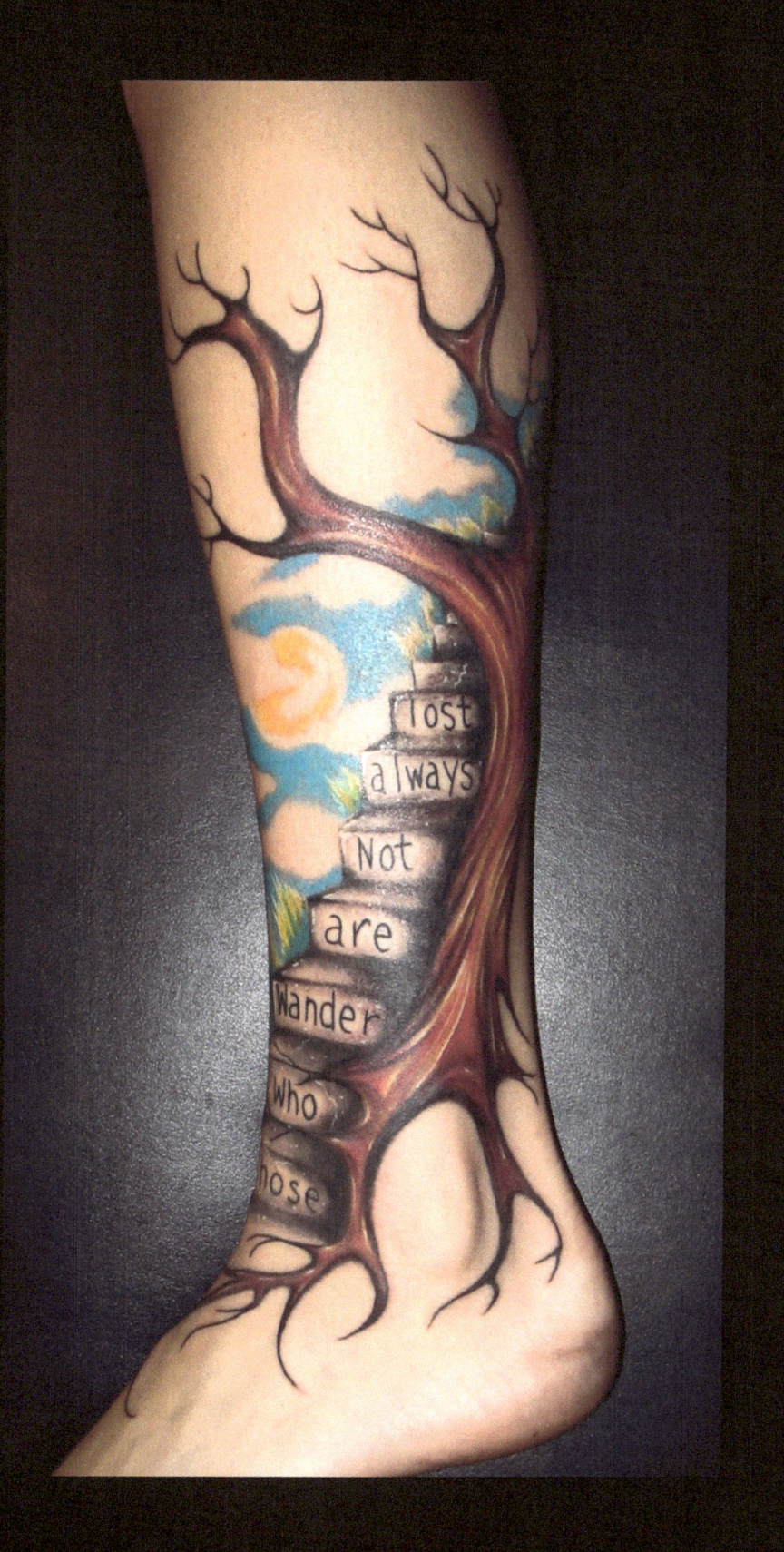

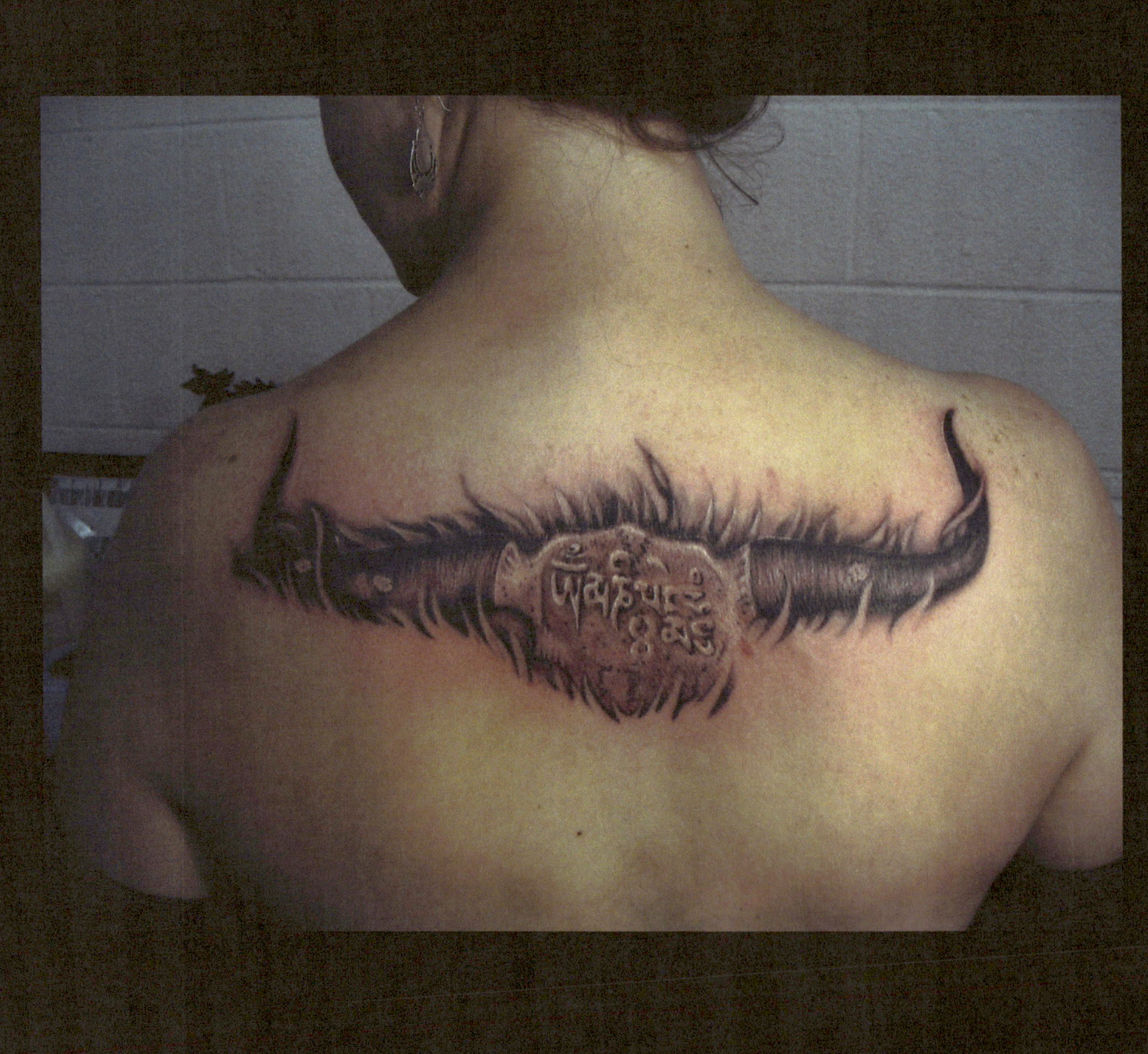

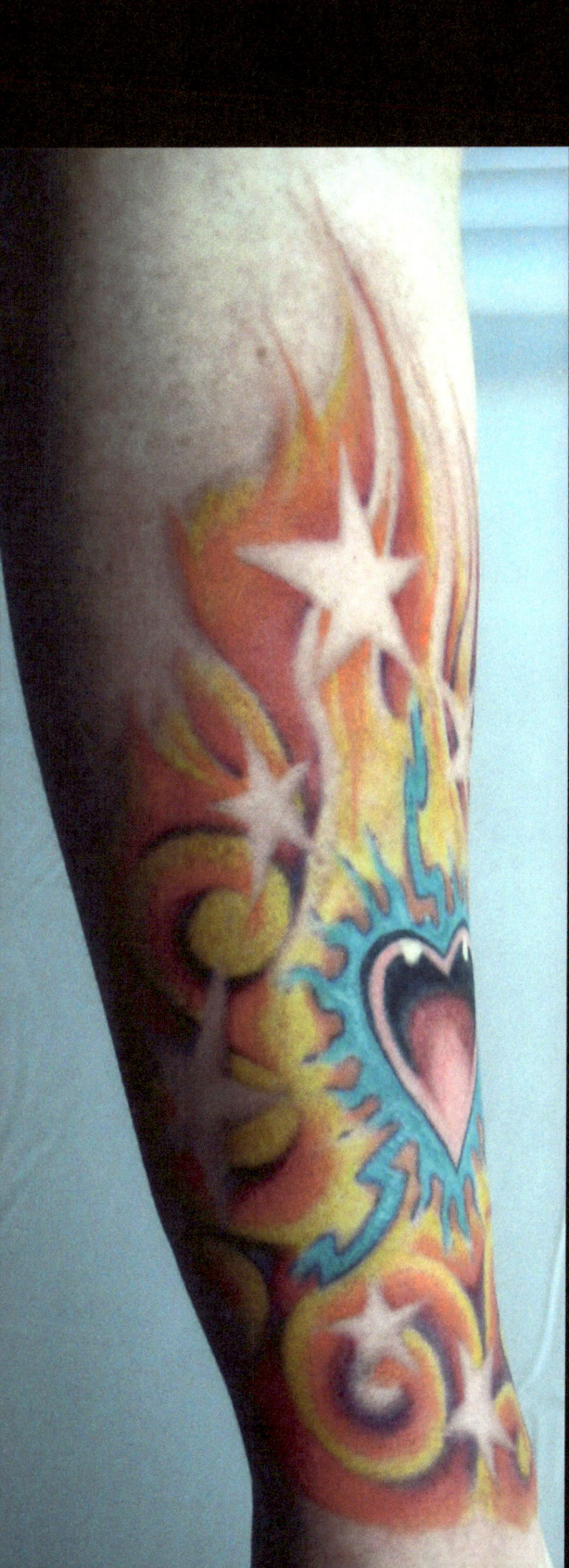

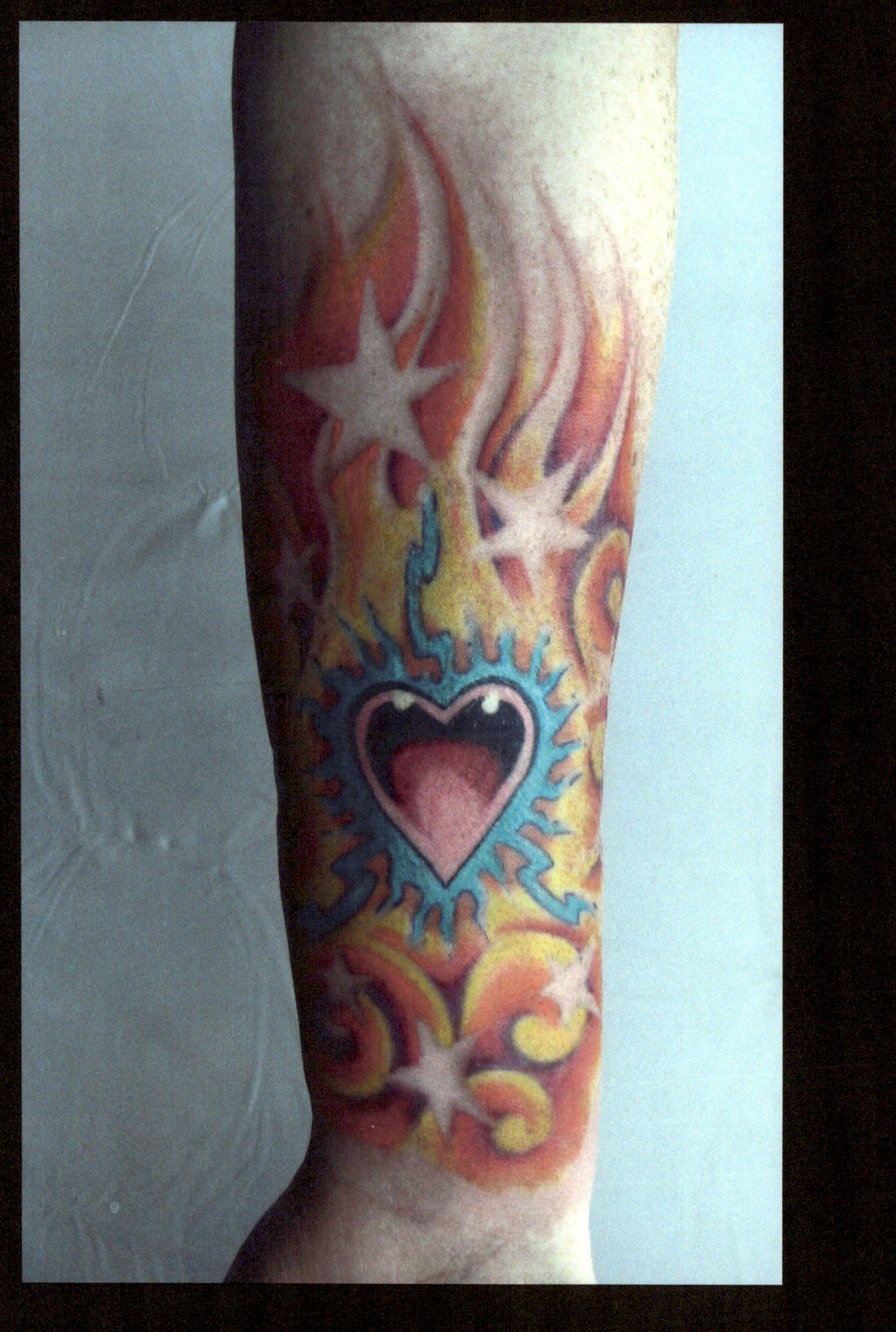

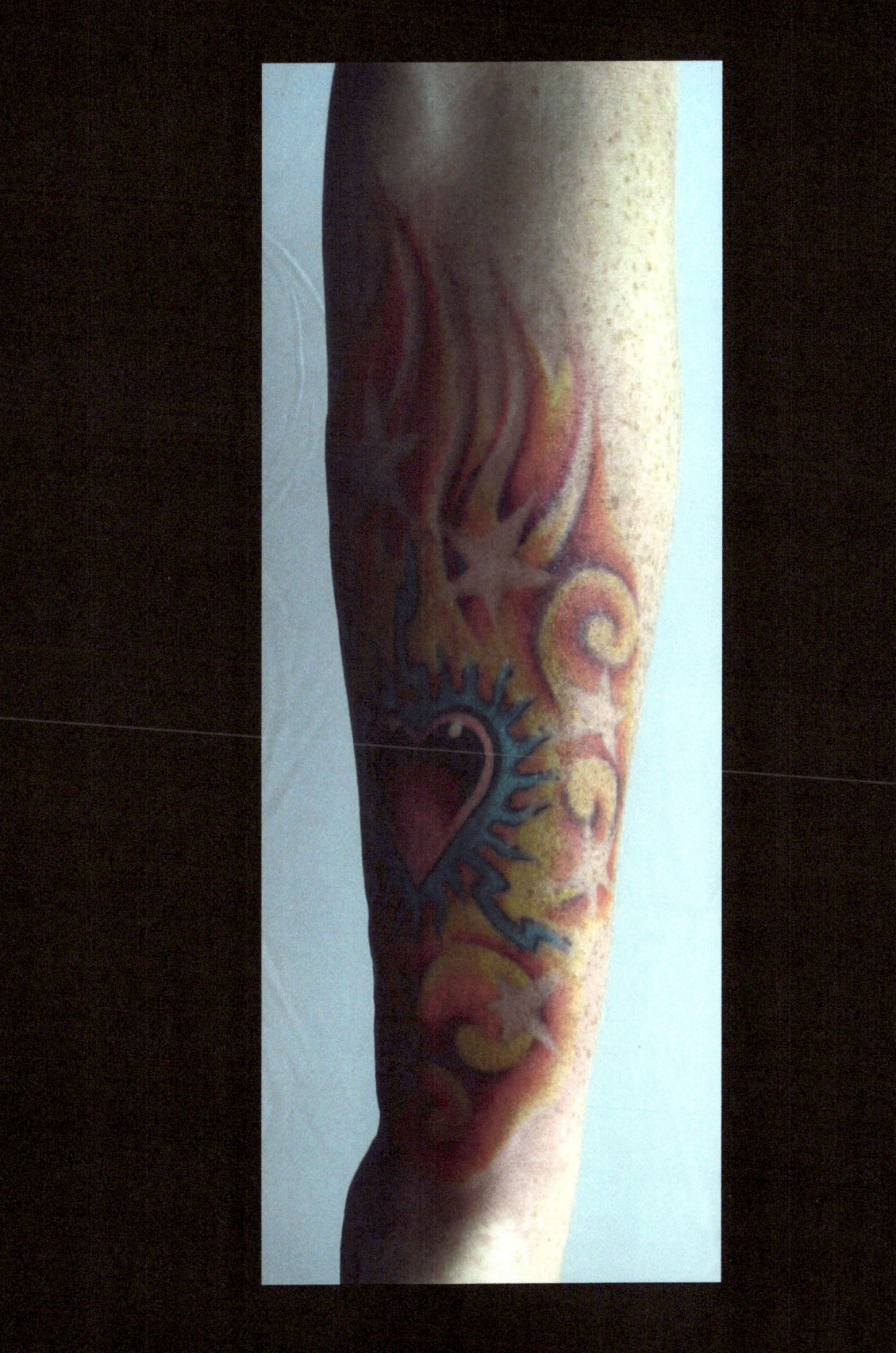

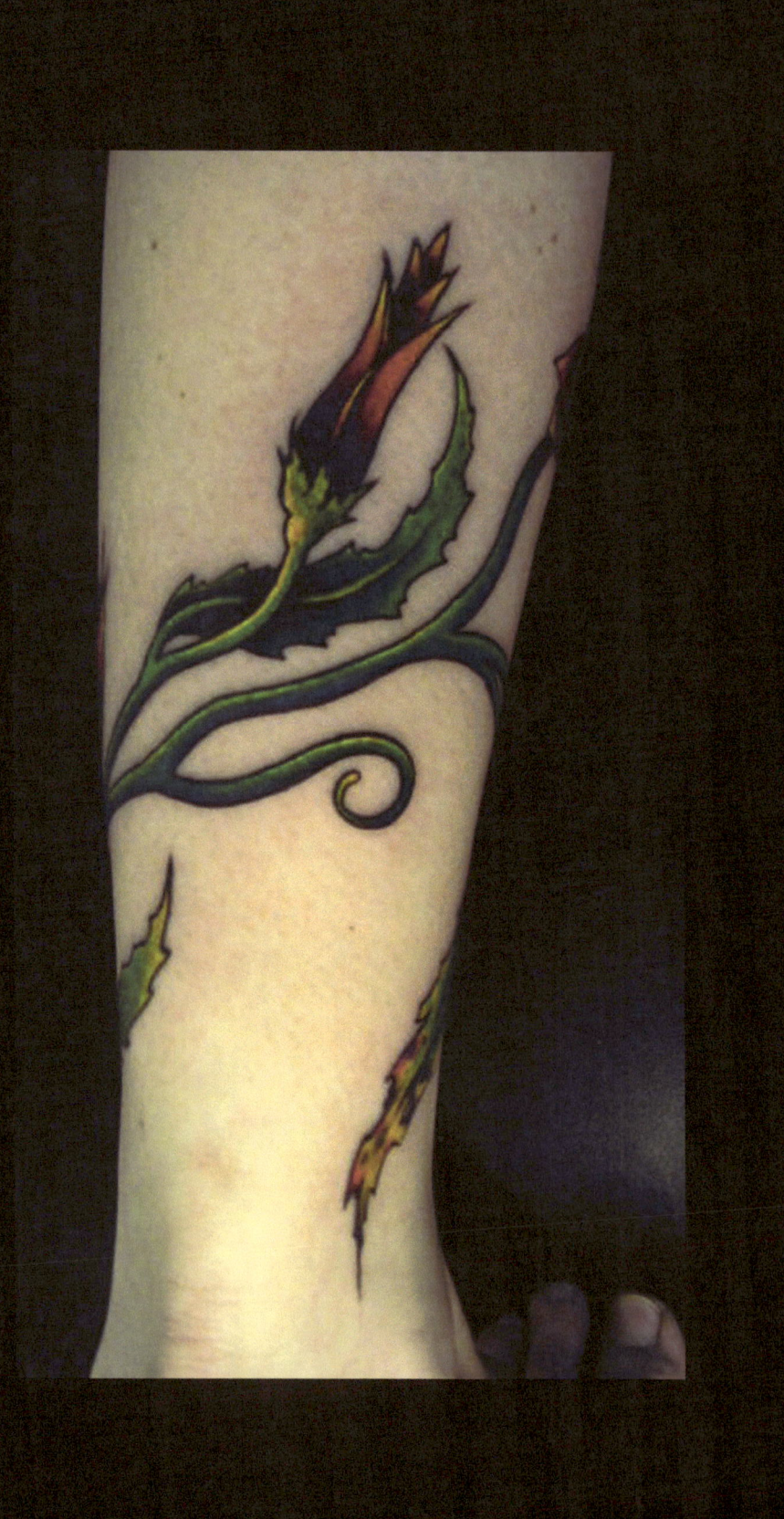

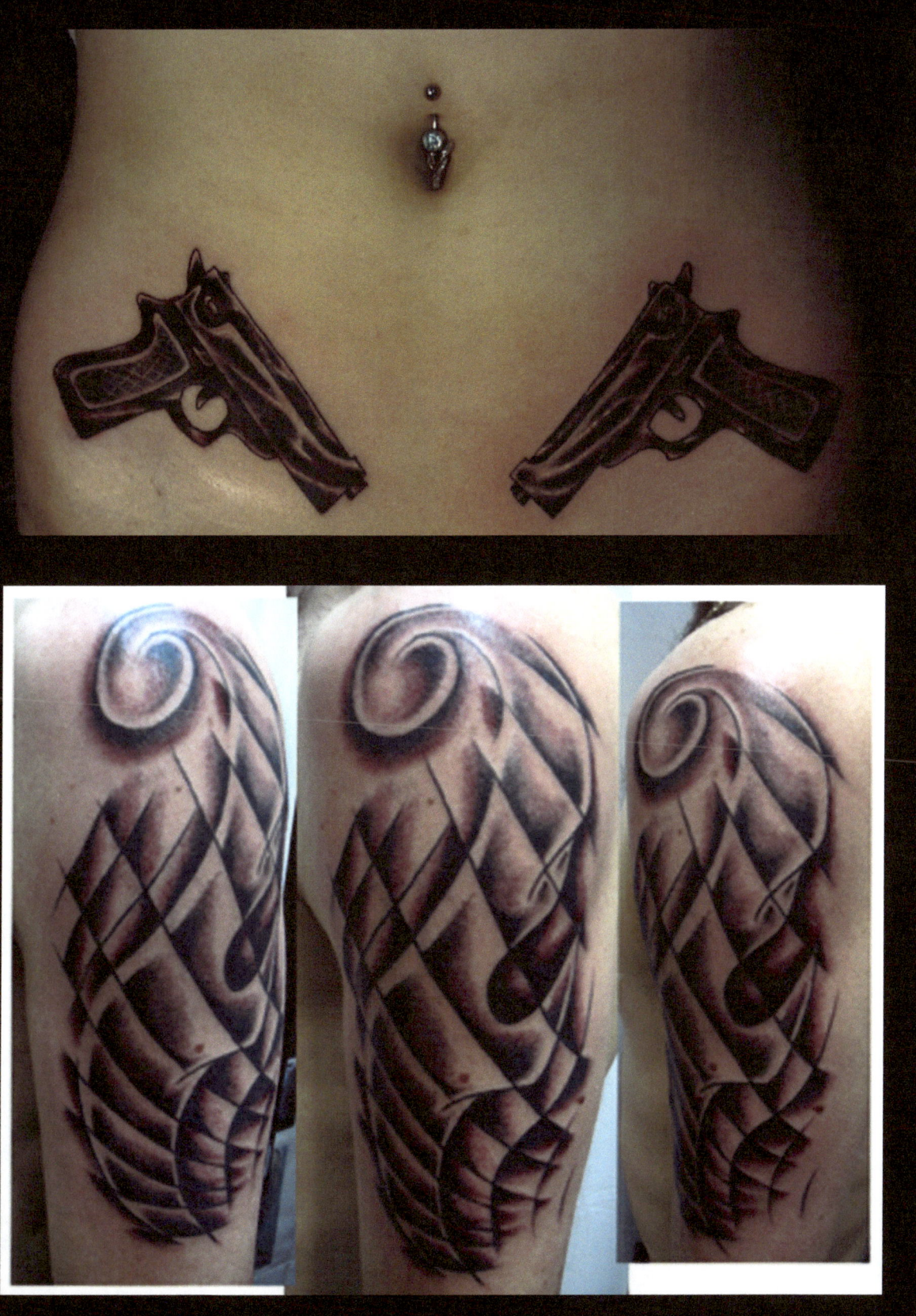

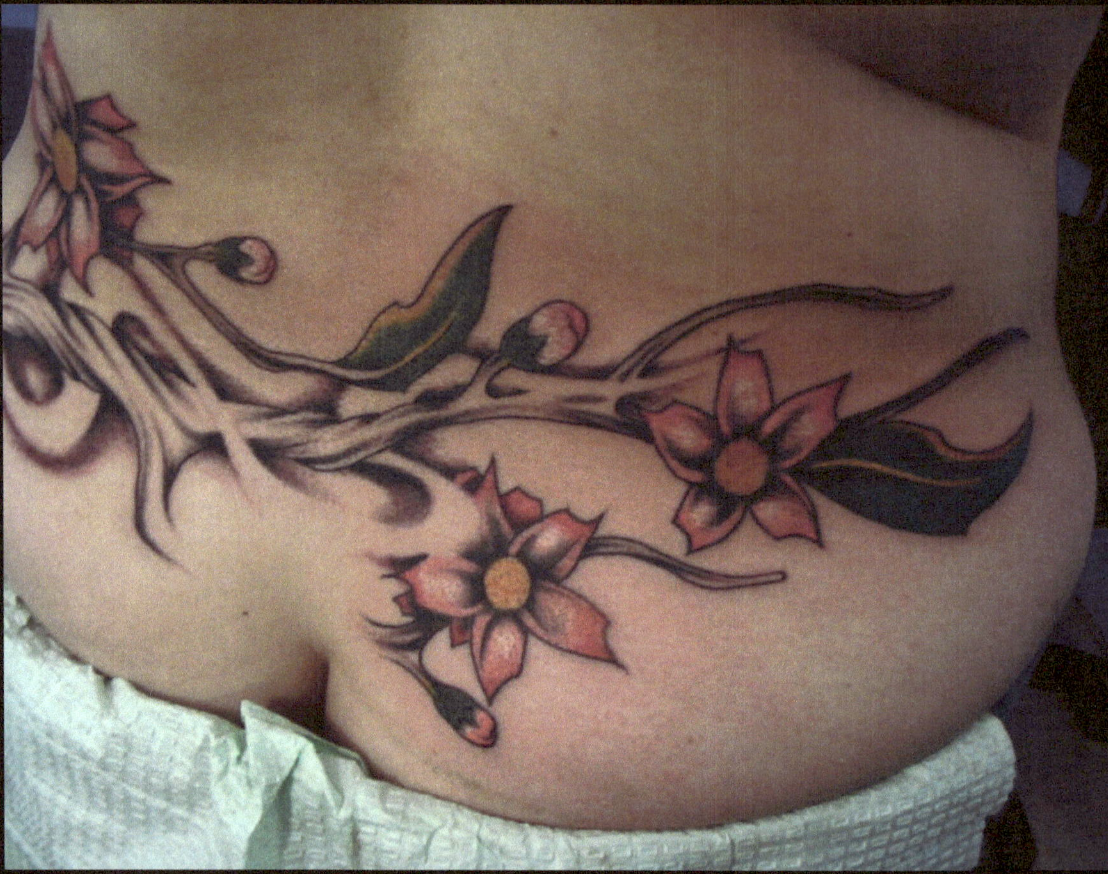

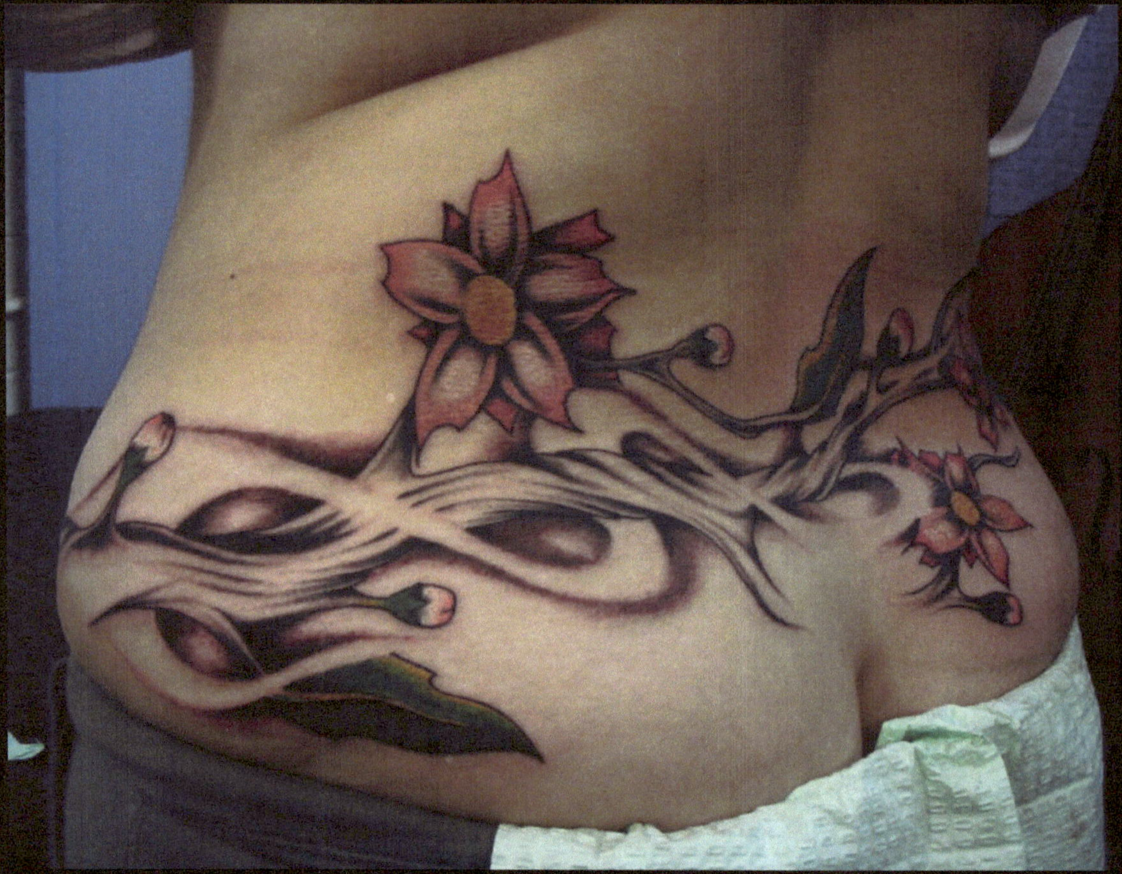

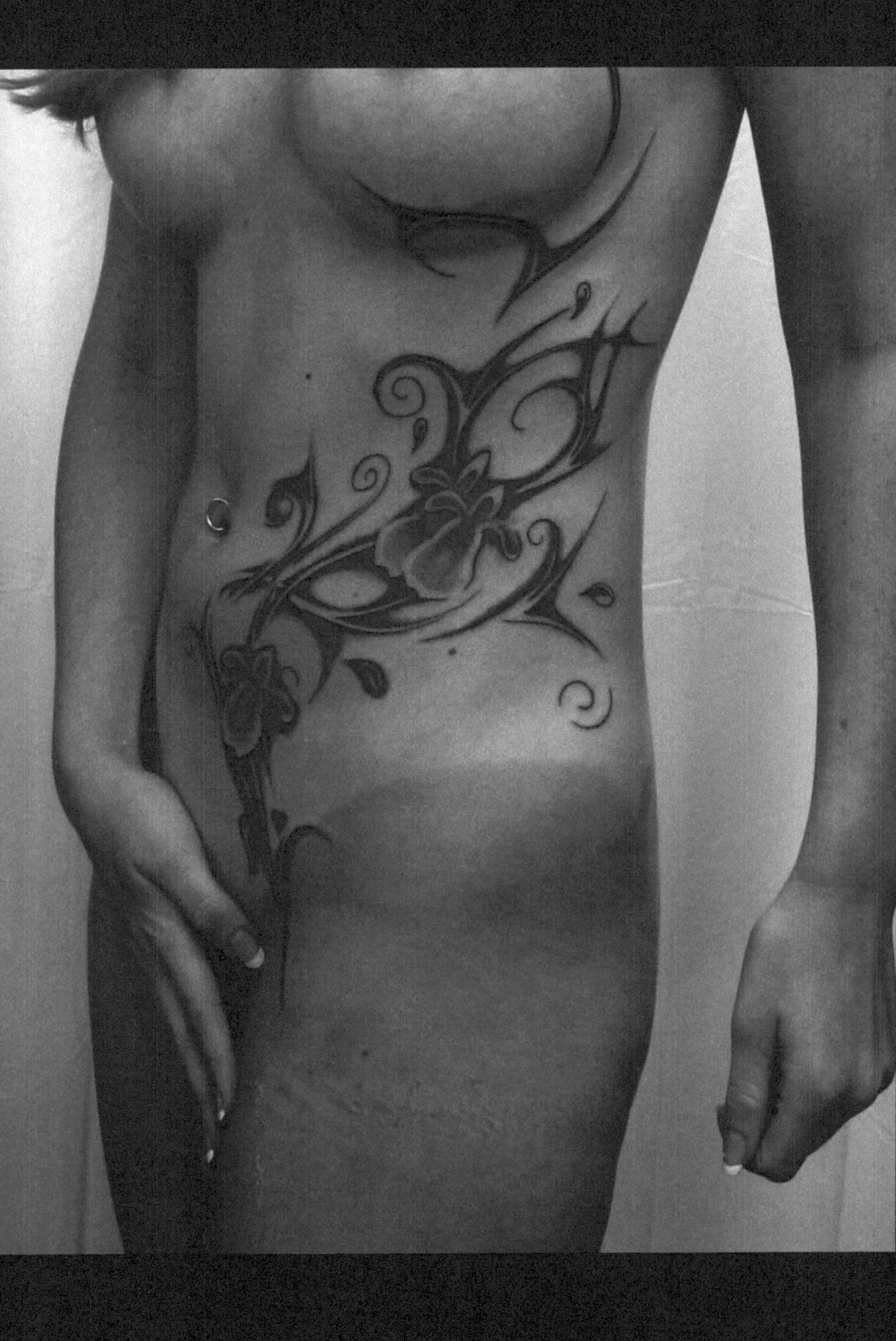

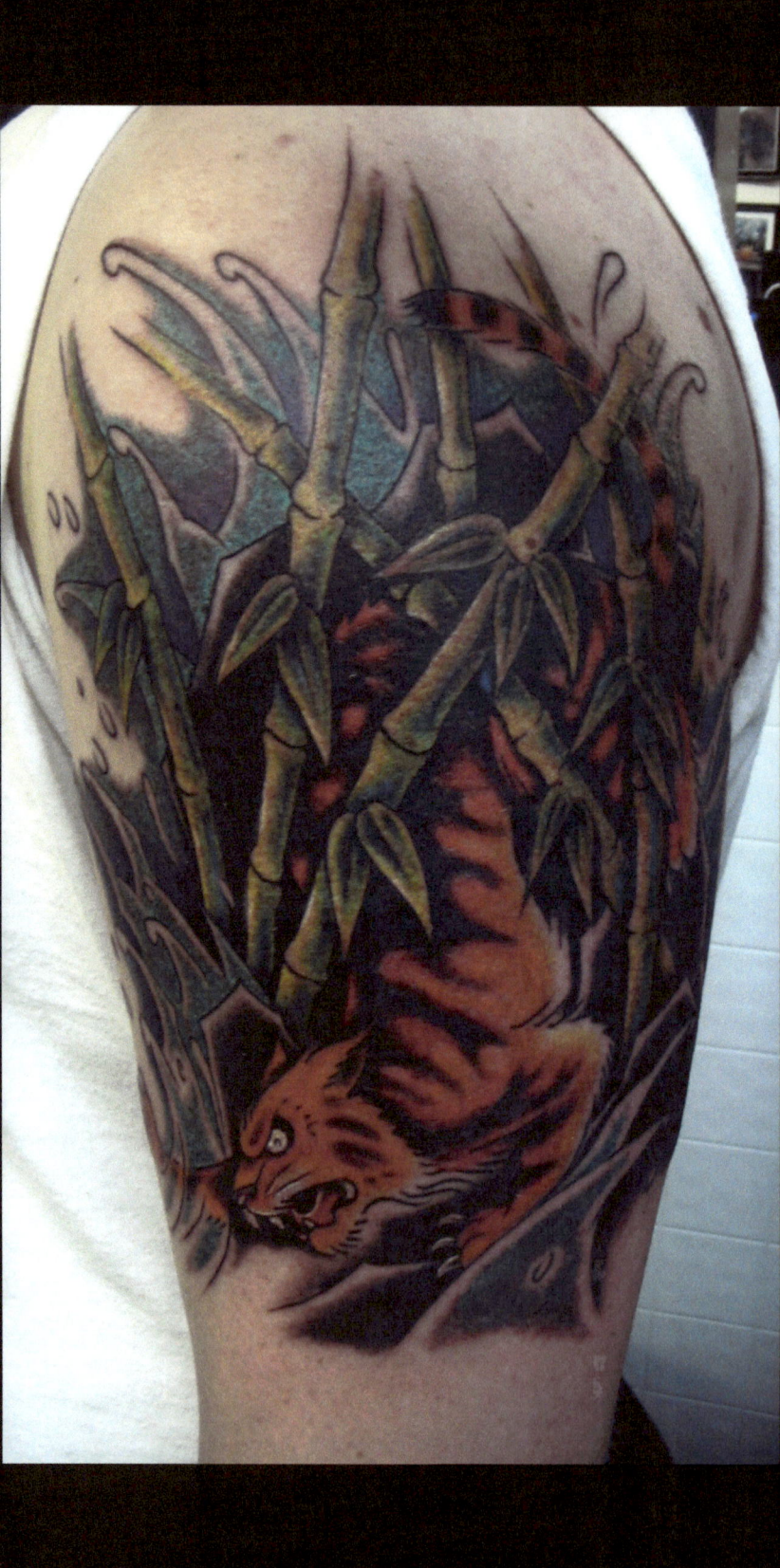

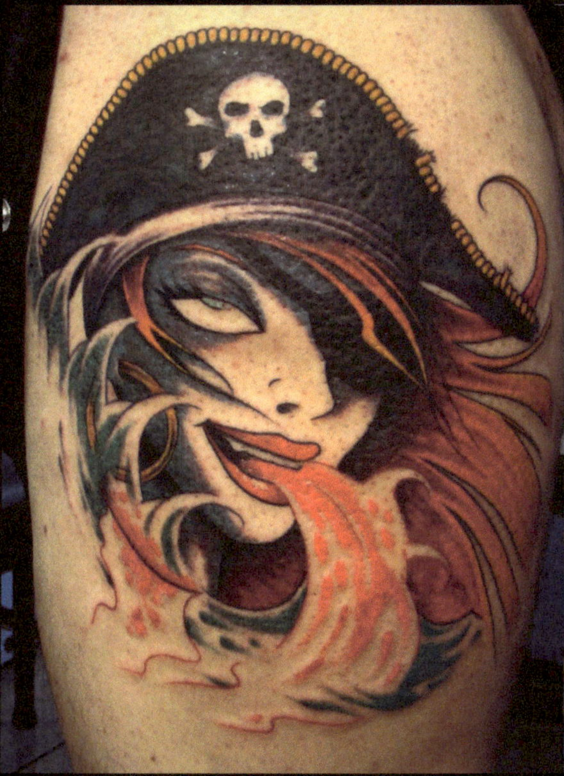
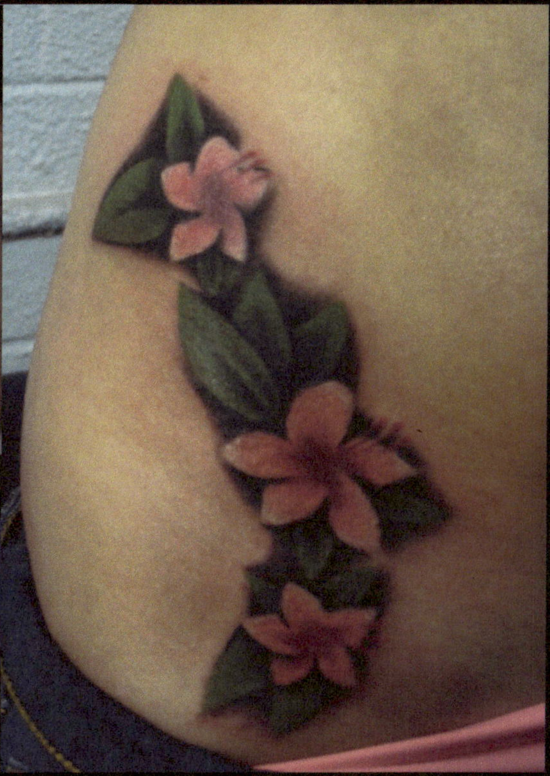
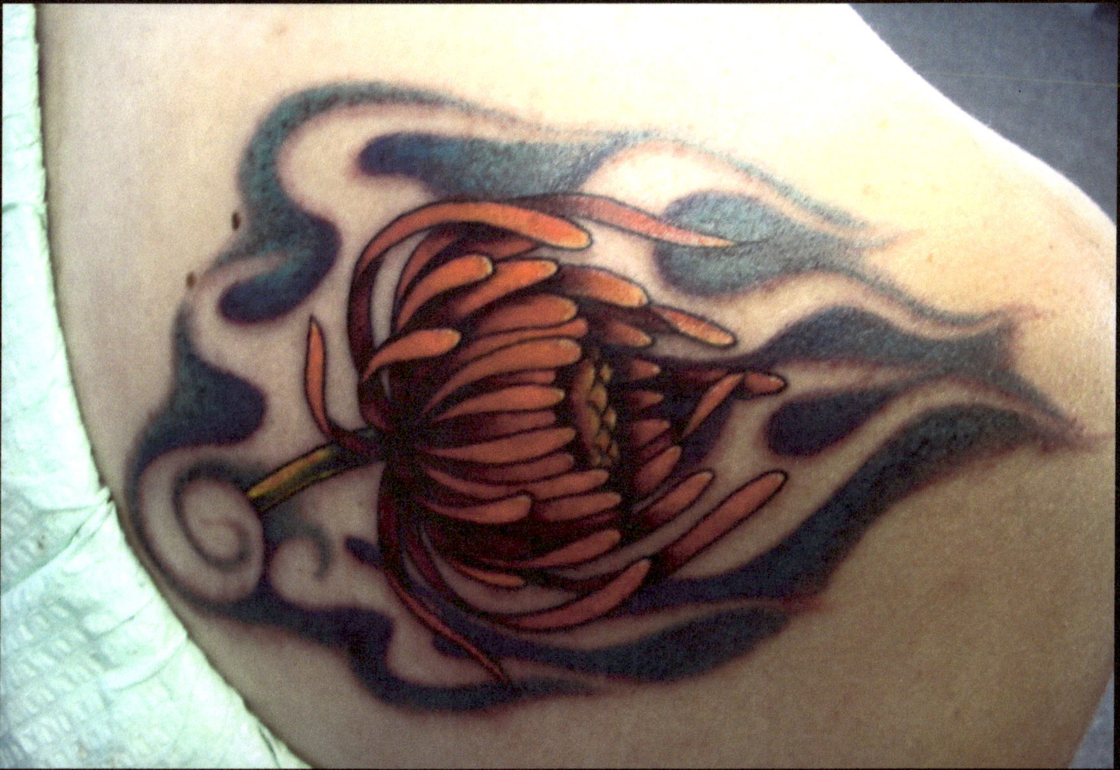

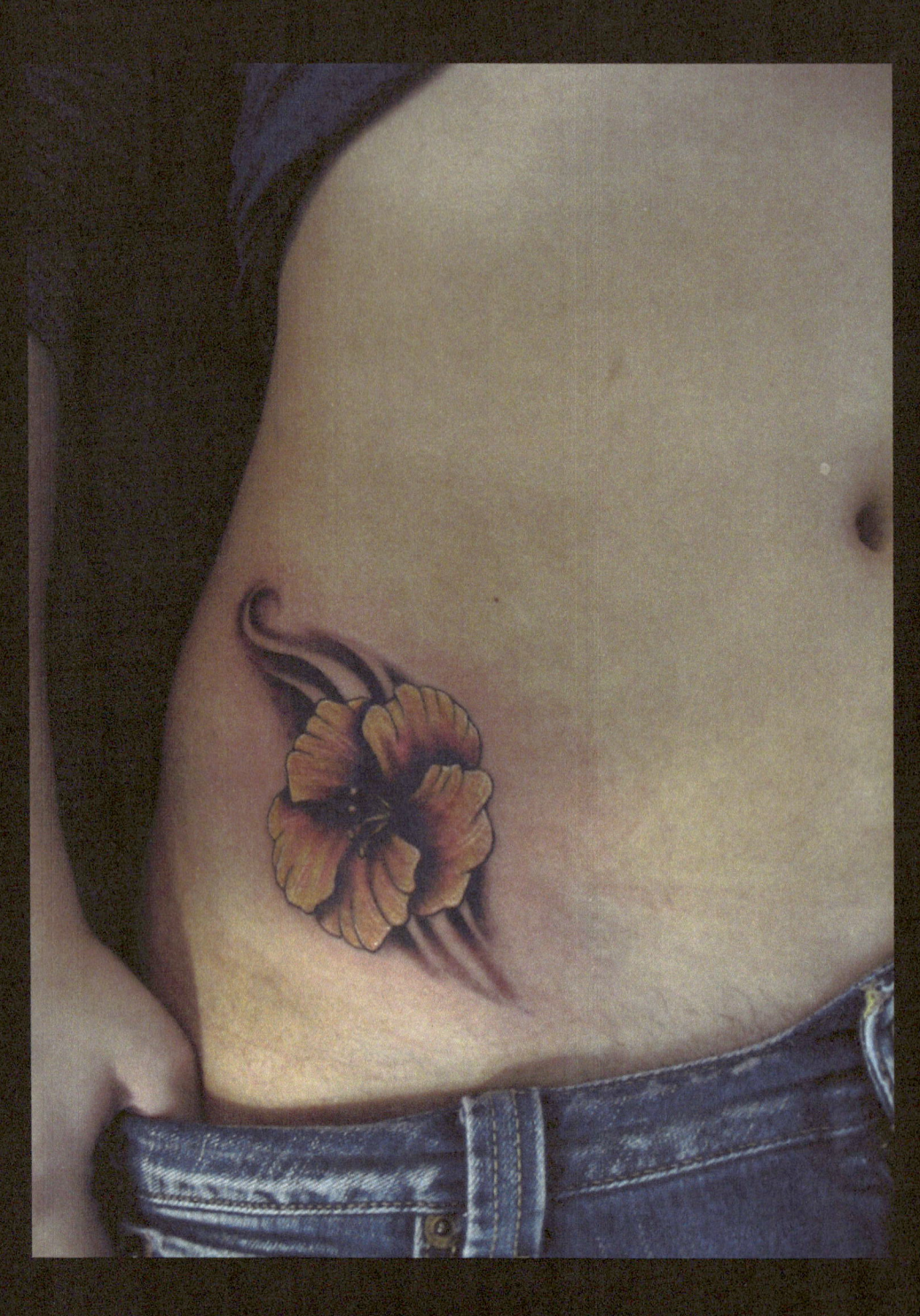

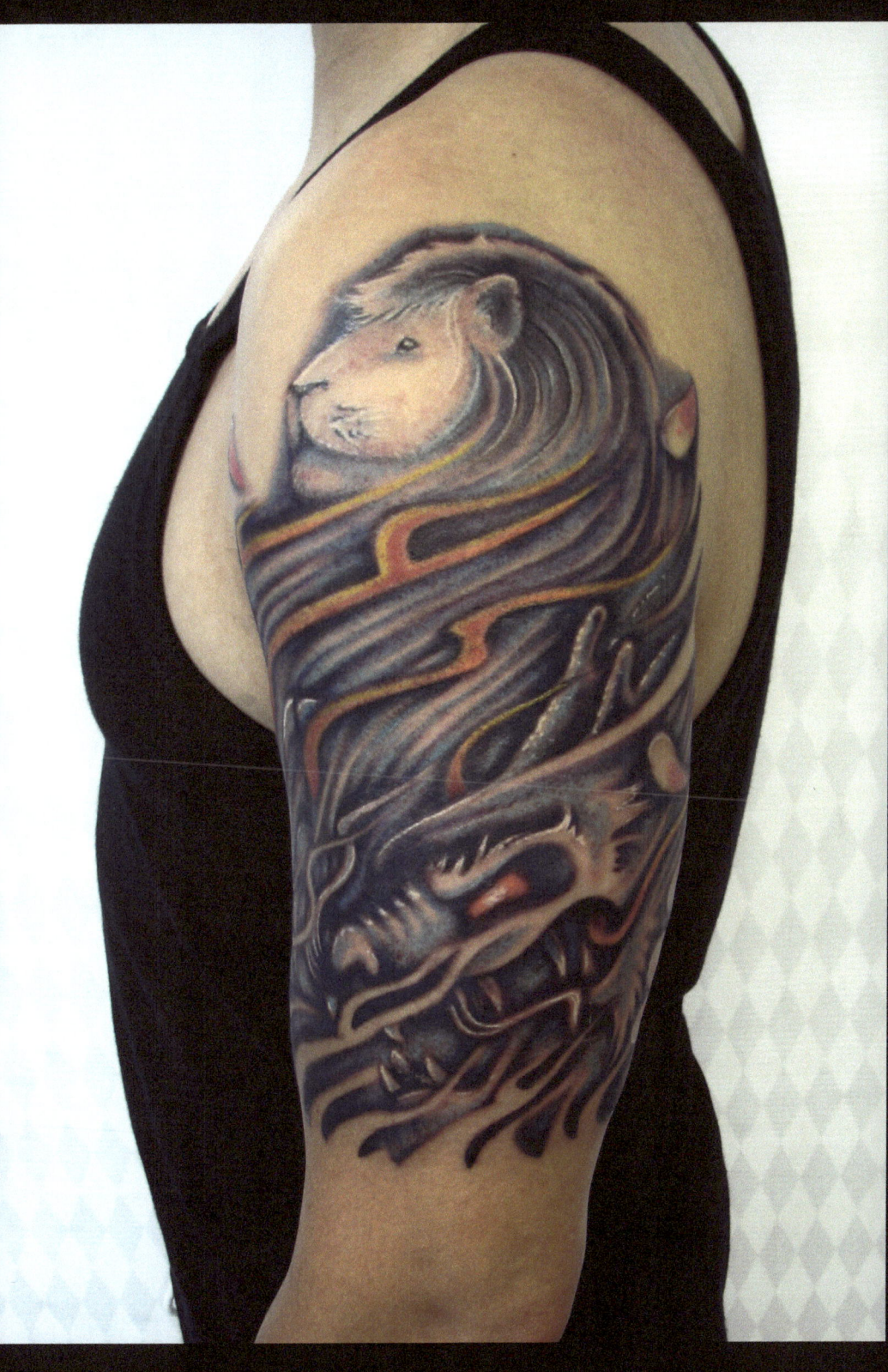

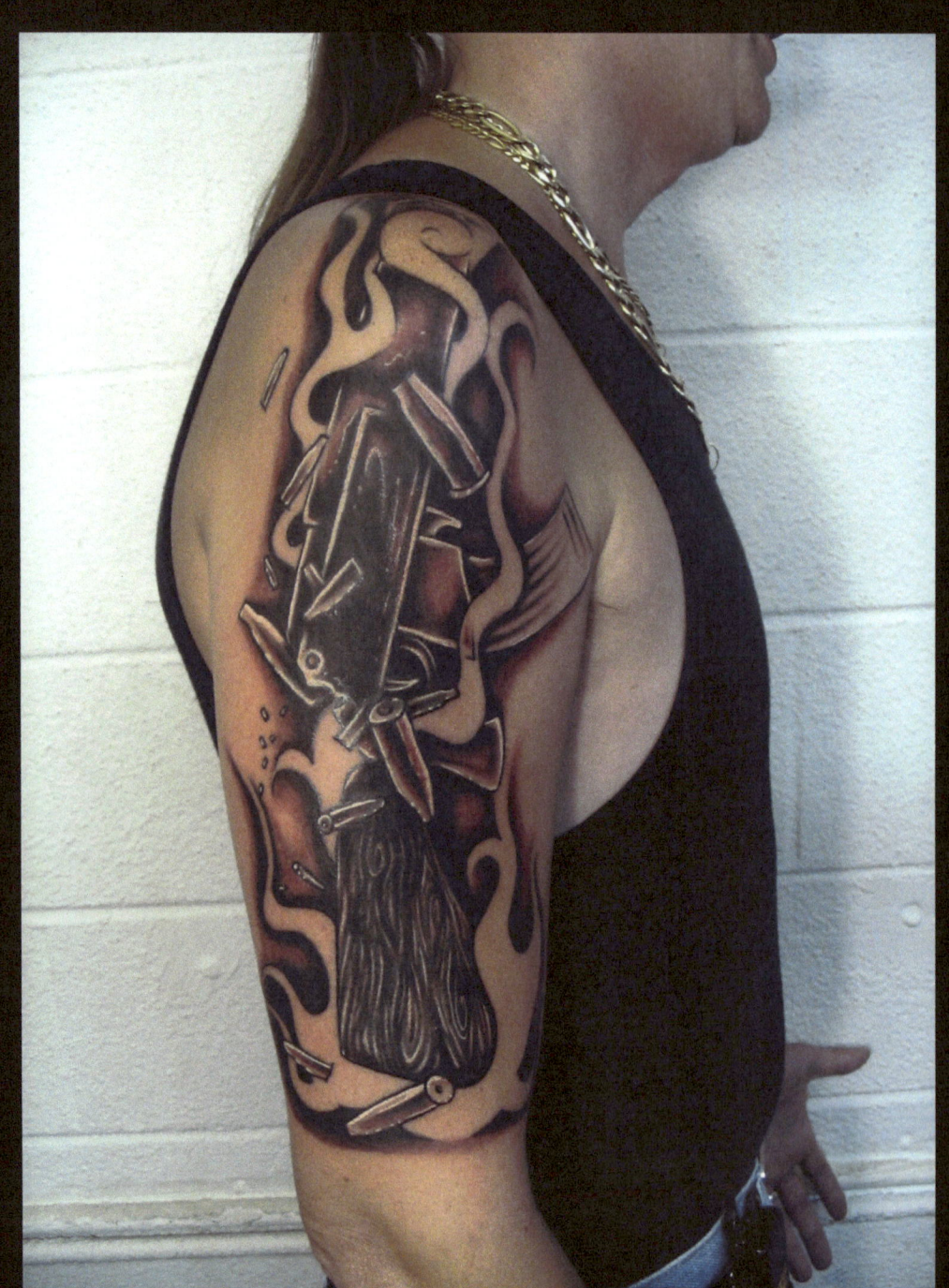

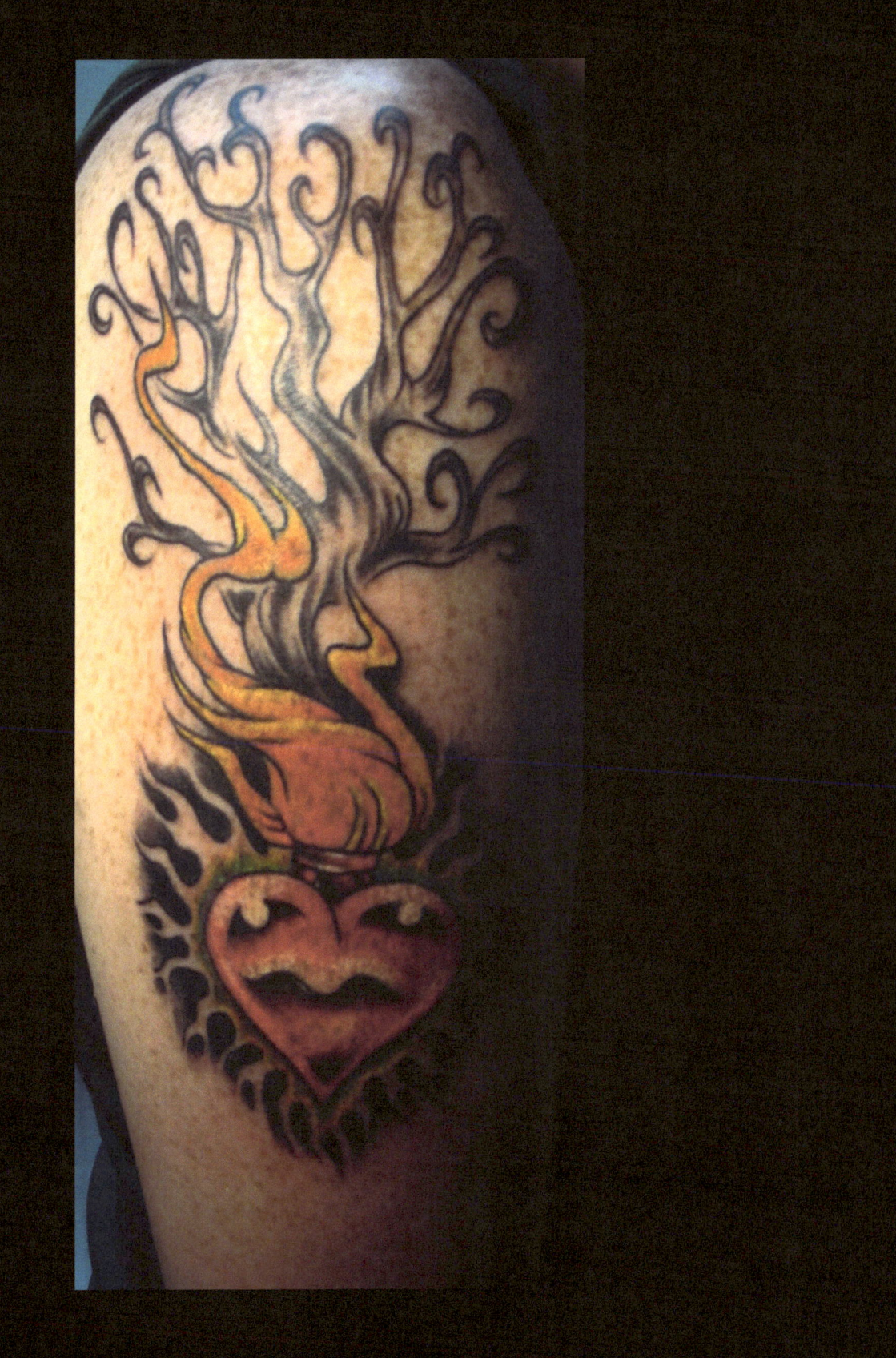

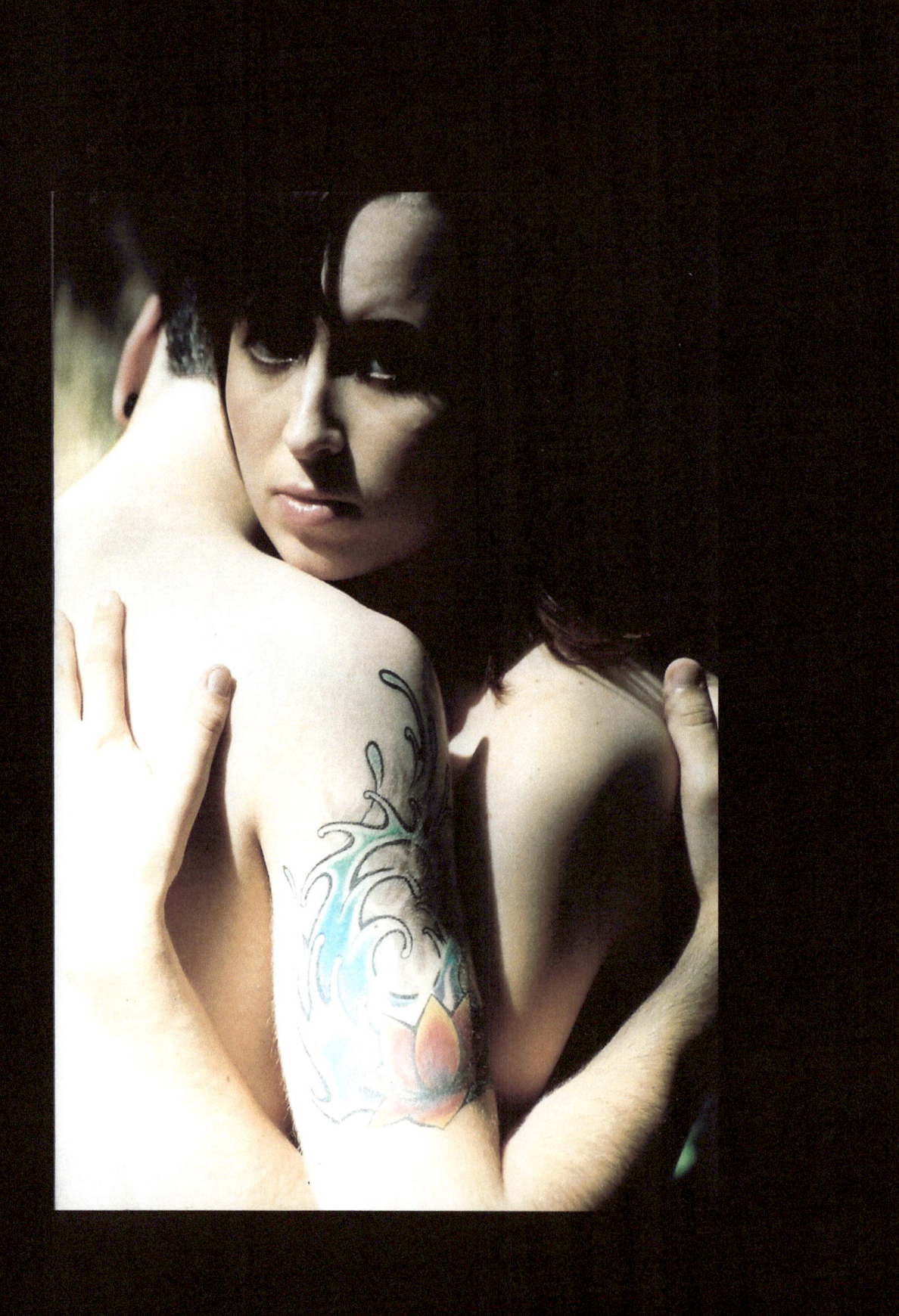

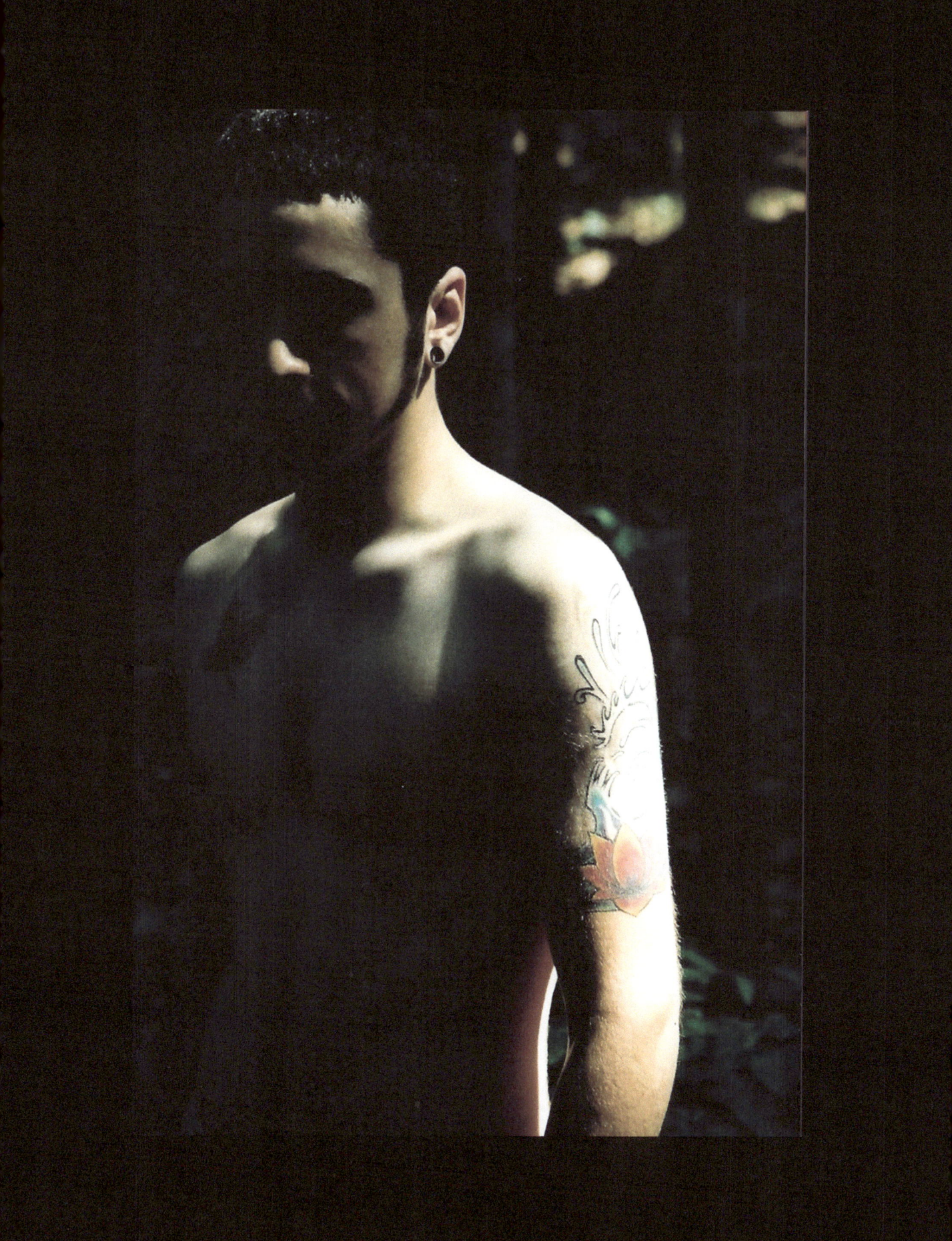

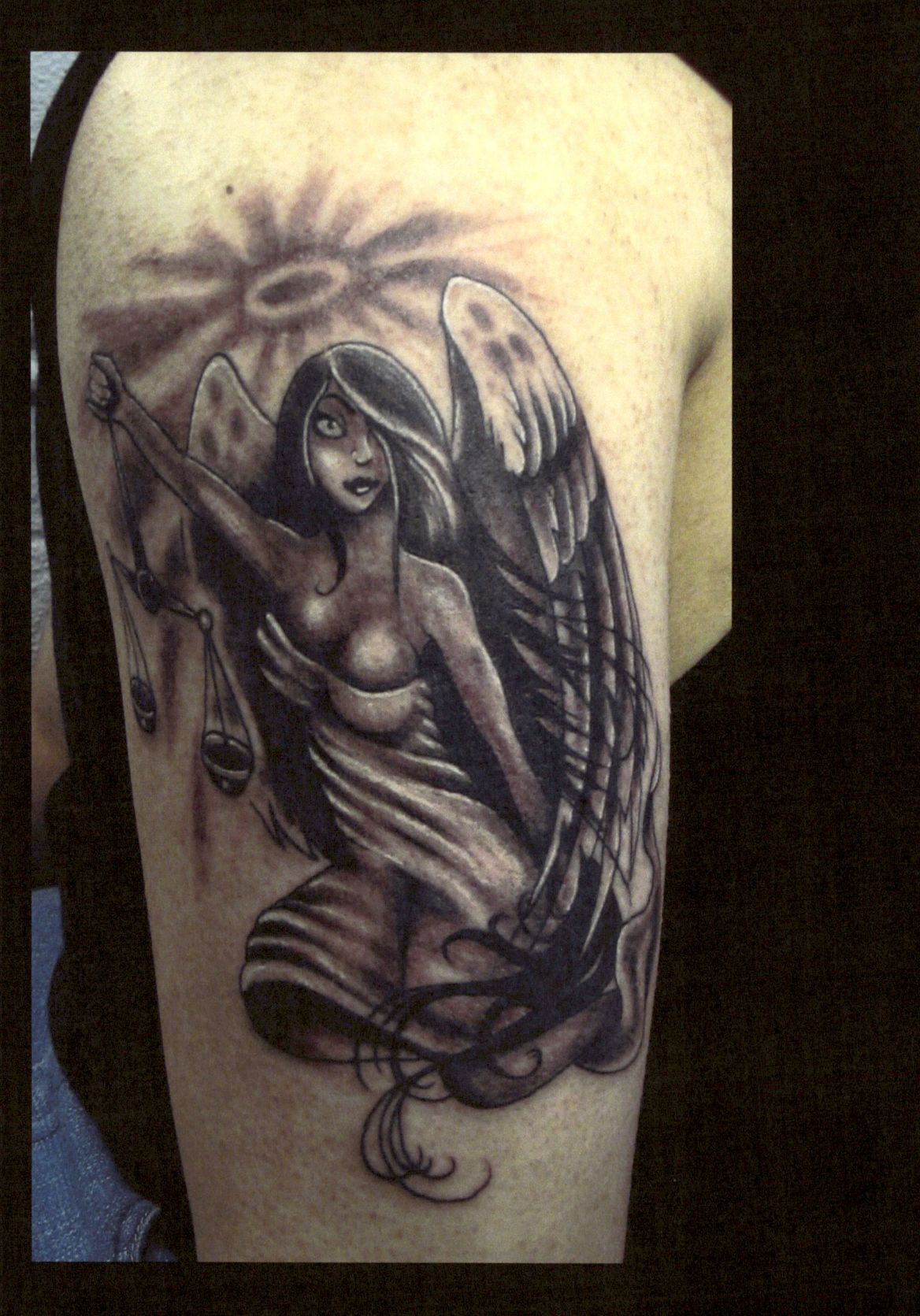

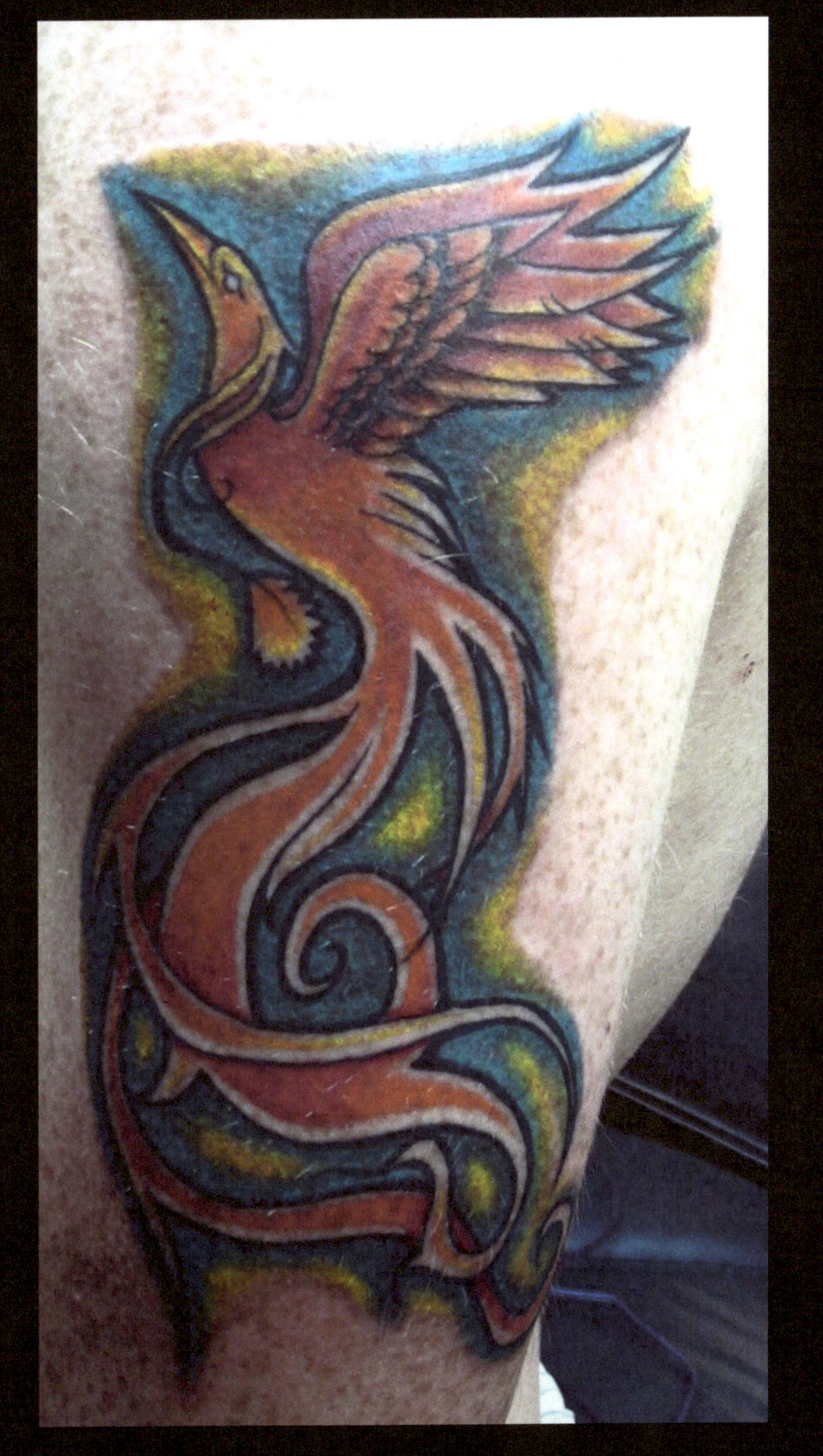

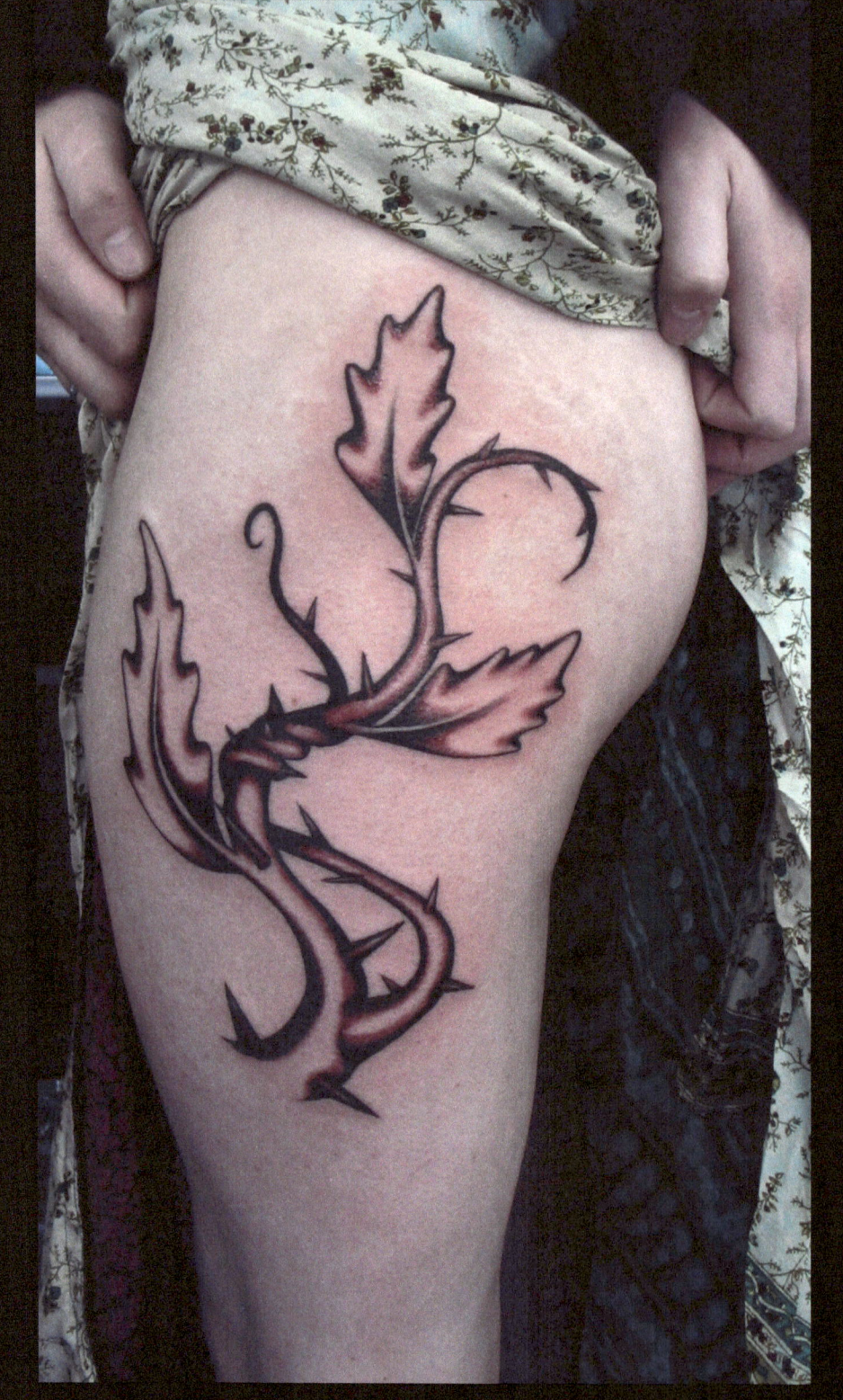

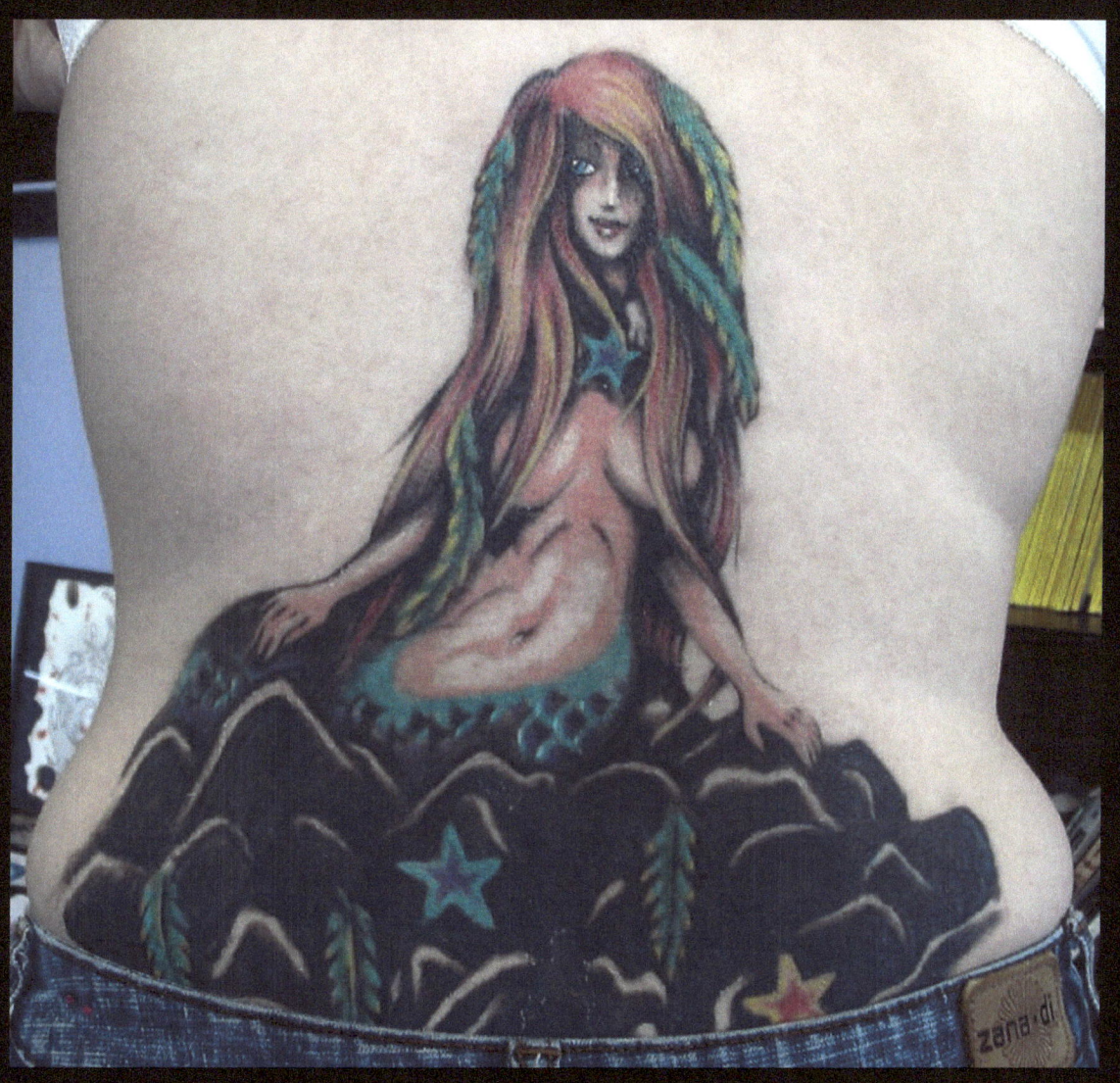

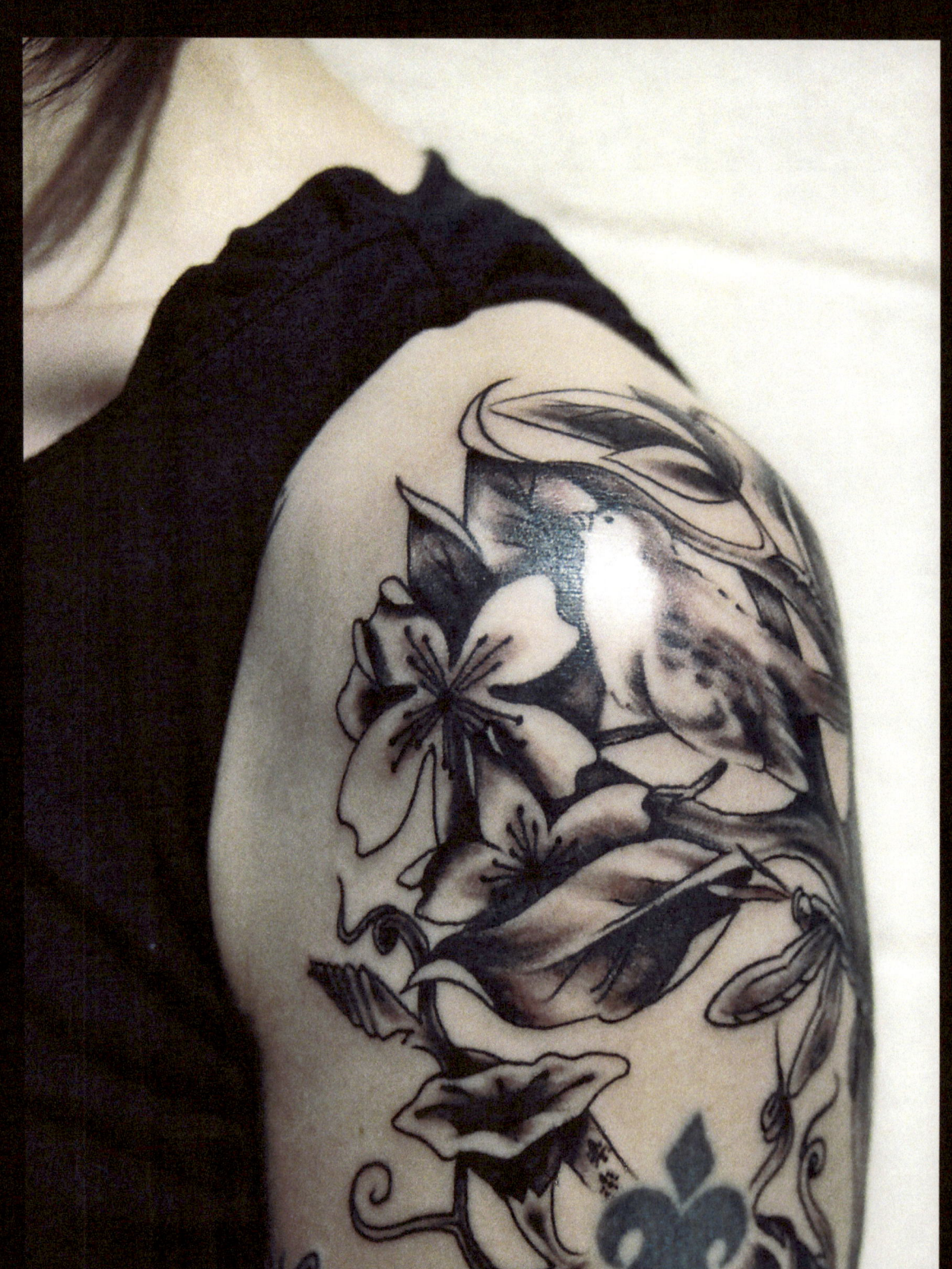

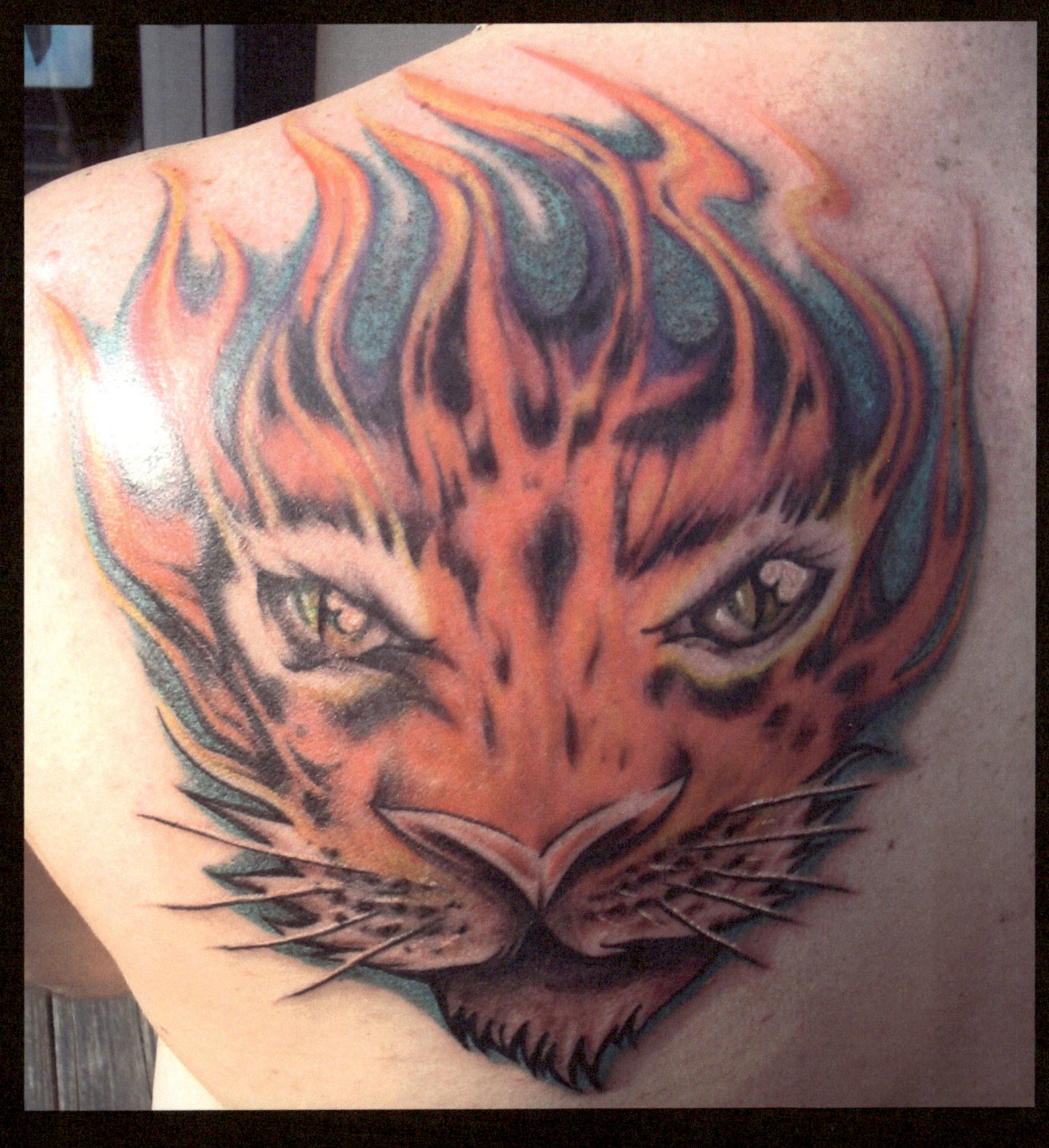

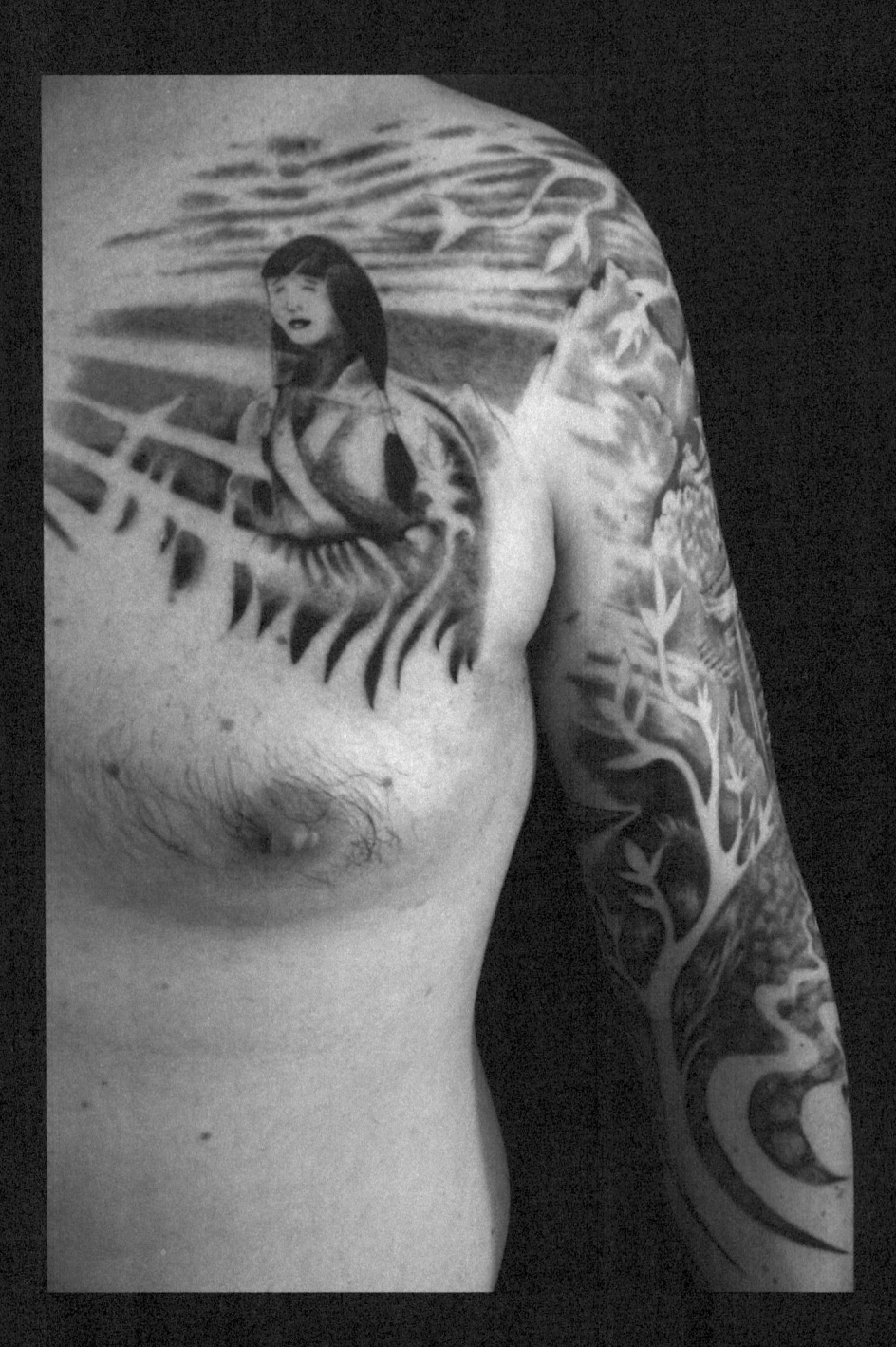

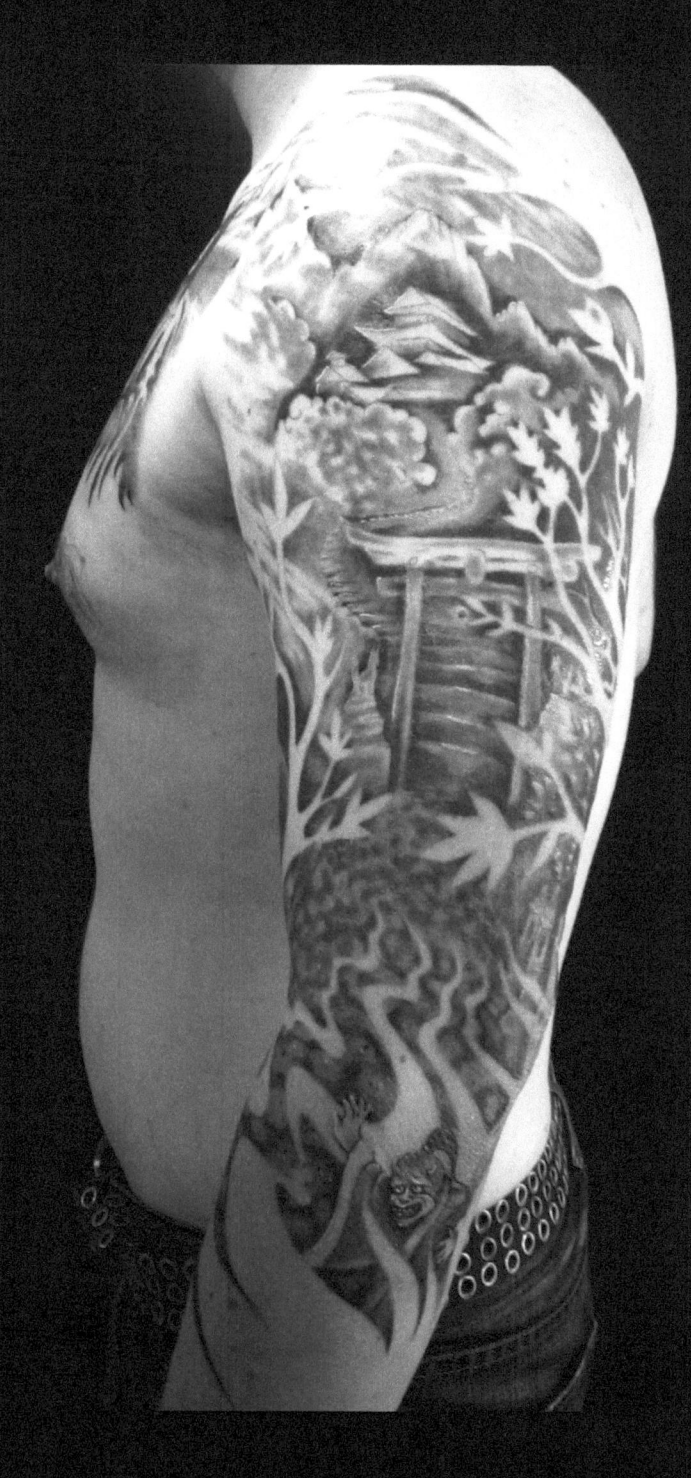

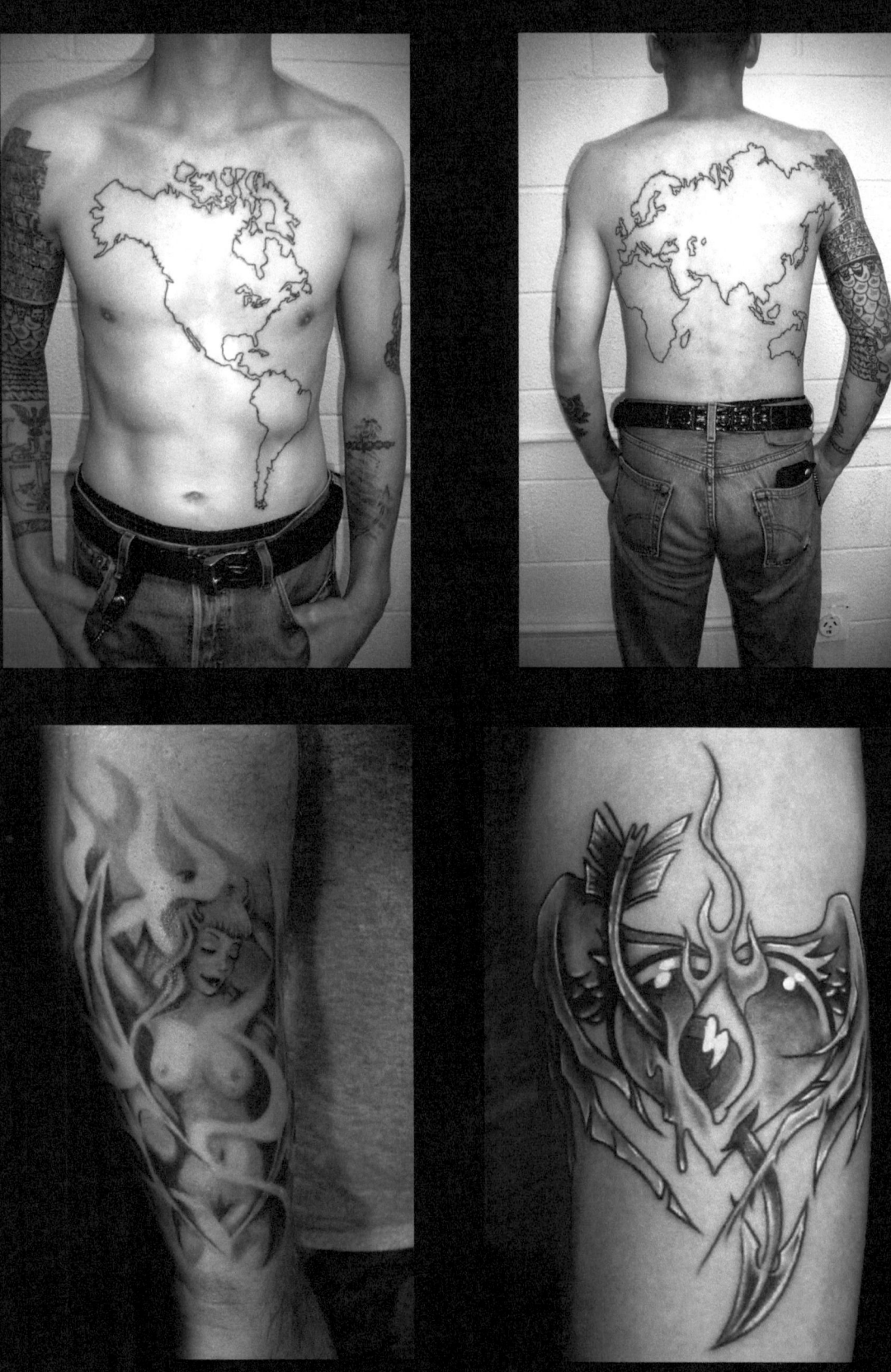

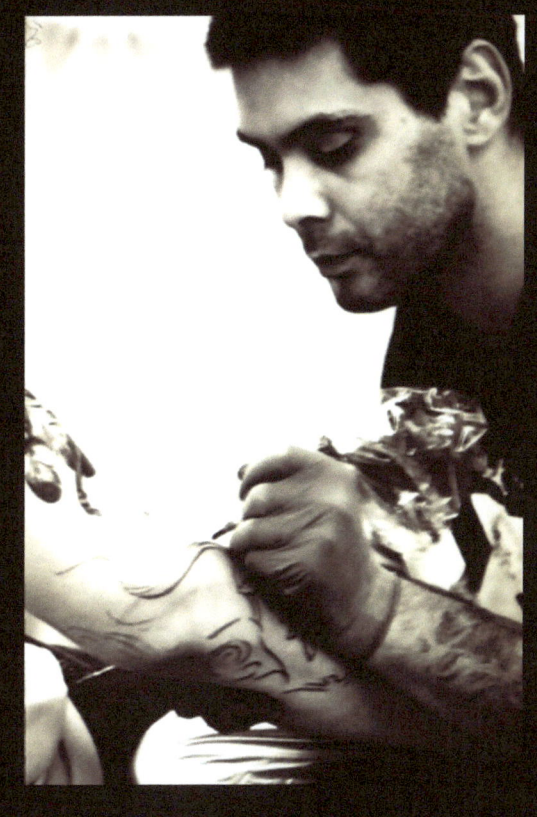

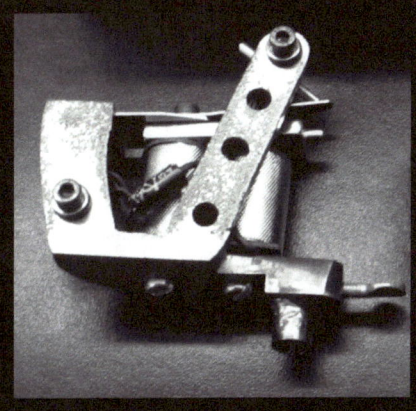

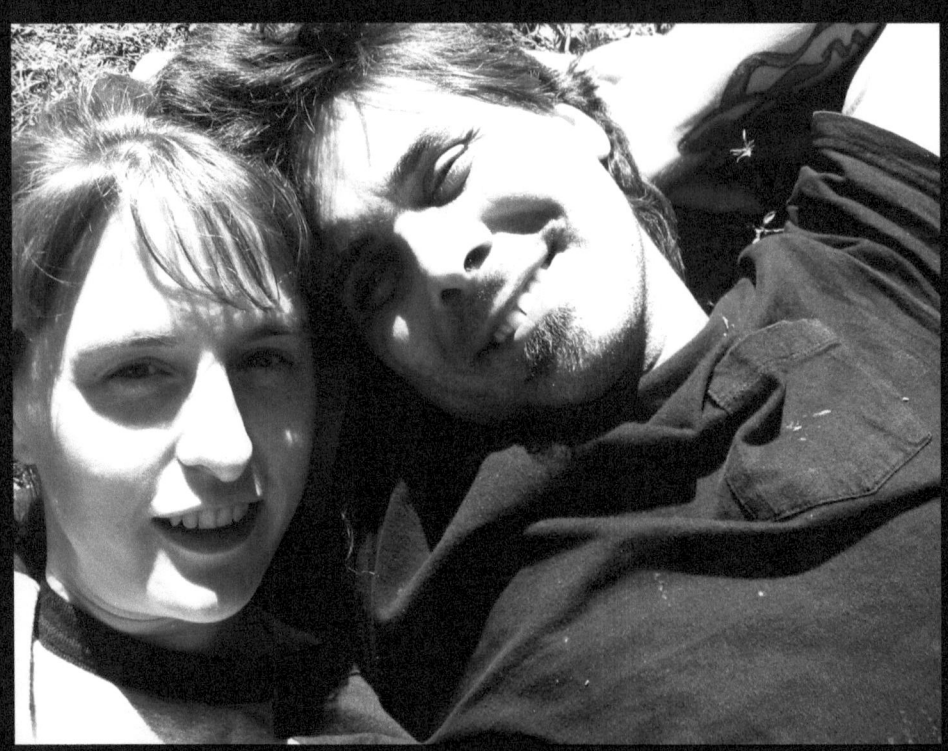